No Country for Black Men

Byron Crawford

In memory of 2Pac and Paul Walker

"All we wanted was a chance to talk.

Instead we only got outlined in chalk."

- D'Angelo

TABLE OF CONTENTS

01.
No More Lonely Nights

"Start envisioning a world where WOMEN FEAR YOU."
— Elliot Rodger

In one of the videos on Elliot Rodger's YouTube account, he sits in a parked car and watches a couple make out on a park bench. He seems deeply upset, and I can't blame him.

PDA is gross... except in cases where the chick is hot and either she isn't aware or she doesn't seem bothered that you're standing there watching her get it on, in which case it's kinda awesome; it's like free, 3-D pron. But how often is that the case, really?

Typically, PDA takes the form of homeless people, or borderline homeless people, dry humping on playground equipment while taxpayers try to tire out their kids so they won't make as much noise—a technique advocated by the dog whisperer, Cesar Milan, albeit for dogs rather than kids.

You see a lot of that sort of thing when you have to move to a less fortunate area due to bad decision making in the years after you graduated from college. People who live in neighborhoods like the one my house in a shanty town is in sometimes live eight or ten to a 1,000 sq-ft house, and so they have to go outside to get it in, drink malt liquor and fortified wines, shout into '90s-style cordless phones and what have you.

If Elliot Rodger had a gun on him that day, he might have popped a cap in that couple's conjoined ass. Instead he just made an angry YouTube video using his cell phone. Those people don't know how lucky they are—unless they saw the video on the news after Rodger's rampage in Isla Vista, CA, which I'm sure would have been awkward. That guy, in particular, won twice that day.

You know how moms are on Facebook. They stay logged on 24-7-365, looking for any wrongdoing in which you might be involved, as well as any image macros with banal aphorisms they can share with distant relatives.

That's why a lot of kids these days don't even fuxwit Facebook. They use those apps where you can send people pictures of your junk and hopefully it doesn't leak to the Internets for the entire world to see. Though from what I understand, some guy has all of those pics and is going through them "as we speak" looking for ones that are especially fapworthy.

There's billions of them, so it might take a while. It might be necessary to create software to sort through them. This is how the future is being built. In the '60s, a lot of our best inventions, including Tang and Astronaut Ice Cream, came from NASA. Mark Zuckerberg, meanwhile, built Facebook to creep on girls at Harvard who didn't want to have anything to do with him.

Elliot Rodger's mom saw his YouTube videos and called the police. Or she may have contacted his shrink, who called the police. That wasn't clear to me from the vast amount of research I did before I began writing this chapter, most of which consisted of reading articles that were hastily thrown together in the hours following Rodger's rampage, for SEO purposes. No one goes back and fixes these things or investigates any further. That's how the Internets news cycle works.

I do happen to know, from watching the entire run of HBO's In Treatment, that if your shrink thinks you might commit a mass shooting, they have to call the cops on you. That's one of the reasons I don't go to a shrink, in addition to the fact that I'm not crazy. I might get in there and start saying all kinds of shit, and I don't wanna have to worry about the guy (or girl!), calling the cops on me. Really, a shrink shouldn't be fielding calls from the parents of a grown-ass man, regardless of who's paying the bill, the same way the cops shouldn't be able to call your parents when you have to spend the night in a drunk tank in college.

5-0 showed up to Elliot Rodger's door to perform what's known as a wellness check. Sometimes a neighbor will order a wellness check on the elderly, if they haven't been seen for a few years and there's a weird smell emanating from the house. Sometimes the cops show up and find the person dead, sitting in front of the TV, which is still on after over a year. Which makes me wonder if the electric company is just bullshitting when they threaten to cut your lights off for nonpayment. I've yet to have someone from the electric company come out and cut off my own lights, a good 15 years into my adulthood, so to speak, but I'm thinking it can't just be some ol' bullshit, because I've seen people get their lights cut off for nonpayment, in the movie Hoop Dreams. Maybe they only cut your lights off if you're black. #BlackLightsMatter

Elliot Rodger answered the door, thus confirming that he was alive, and he told the cops there was no need for them to be concerned, so they didn't bother searching his apartment. That may have been the most difficult aspect of this entire thing for me to accept. No disrespect to anyone who lost their lives. I'm just saying.

The irony of 5-o not checking Elliot Rodger's apartment for a weapons cache is that, for people who haven't been rotting alone for weeks on end or eaten by their many cats, the term wellness check is more or less synonymous with gun confiscation. Otherwise, what's the point of sending the police to check on someone who's clearly not dead, I mean if they're uploading videos to YouTube? These are cops we're talking about, not doctors; not only do they not know medicine, they barely know how to read and write. They have no way of assessing your state of well-being.

A while back, the National Guard introduced a training exercise that involved going door to door, searching people's houses and taking their guns, in the wake of, say, a natural disaster or a terrorist attack. Members of the National Guard objected to such an exercise, because a lot of people in the National Guard are militia types who joined the National Guard in the first place because they were afraid someone might come and try to take their guns. The National Guard responded by changing the name of the exercise to "wellness checks," though it still involved searching people's houses for guns which they would then confiscate.

The government doesn't want us to have guns because they don't want us to be able to fight back once it's time for them to round us up and put us in FEMA camps.

———

Originally, Elliot Rodger's plan was to shoot up a sorority at the University of California at Santa Barbara over the Halloween weekend in 2013, but he had to push it back some after an incident in which he tried to kill some girls at a house party and ended up falling off of a cliff. I hate when that happens.

Halloween would have been a good weekend to pull a mass shooting at a college. You could probably walk around campus dressed as a school shooter, and people would just think you had an inappropriate sense of humor. You'd have to carry an obviously-fake gun, with an orange plastic tip on the end, lest you get tasered by overzealous campus rent-a-cops (note that you'd have to be white to pull anything like this), but you could keep a few real guns in your backpack.

The day Elliot Rodger did end up trying to shoot up Isla Vista was on a Memorial Day weekend. School may have already been out at that point, and anyway there was no excuse for him to be walking around dressed like Cho Seung-Hui. But let's not get too far ahead of ourselves.

The fact alone that Elliot Rodger was allowed to attend this party should have been viewed as a positive. I suspect that there's a lot of parties that take place without me knowing. This was a rich kids party at a fancy house in the hills; hence there being a cliff for him to fall off of. I've never been to a party at a house on a cliff. Girls go to parties like that to meet guys who have a lot of money. They don't care about the guy's looks, or whether or not he's on the autism spectrum, they're just trying to get "sponsored." Rodger might have been able to score on the basis of ostensibly having a few dollars in his pocket. I wonder if he just didn't try hard enough.

Rodger saw a few girls that he thought he could push over the edge of a cliff. He tried to, and instead he somehow ended up being thrown over the edge of the cliff himself. One of the girls may have known jiujitsu. A lot of girls are taking martial arts right now, because there's a BS moral panic about non-consensual lovemaking in college. They can't do much in the way of real damage, but there's a way they can use your own momentum against you, if you were to, say, try to push them over the edge of a cliff. Really, you shouldn't be trying to toss a girl from a cliff anyway. I can hardly think of a situation in which that would be necessary.

Rodger's leg was busted in the fall, and then he ended up getting his ass kicked in the driveway by a guy who recognized him as the guy who'd just attempted to push several girls over the edge of a cliff. Some "white knight," as they're known on the Internets.

White knights intervene on a girl's behalf because they hope it'll get them some pussy. It hardly ever works, because girls don't like nice guys. Chicks dig jerks. If anything, a girl whom Elliot Rodger didn't try to toss from a cliff might have seen what he did and tried to have sex with him, rationalizing it by telling herself that he would never do that to her. Ted Bundy had many a female admirer, as does James Holmes, the guy who shot up that Batman movie in Colorado.

Elliot Rodger's plan, as described in one of his YouTube videos, was to shoot up the hottest sorority at UCSB. He figured he could just waltz right in and start busting off shots while the girls were in there looking at each other's junk, or whatever it is girls do in sorority houses. He didn't have any way of knowing that sorority houses are on lockdown at all times, like supermax prisons, because he went to a community college, where they don't even have dorms.

Why is it that community colleges are located in nice suburbs near where you already live, where presumably the real estate is pricey, and yet there's never a shortage of parking spaces? Meanwhile, real colleges are located in the middle of nowhere, surrounded by vast expanses of nothingness, like in the movie Fargo, and yet there's never anywhere to park. You could fuck around and end up driving around for two weeks looking for a place to park and then just have to drop out. It's one of the many reasons I don't recommend going to college.

I should point out that before Elliot Rodger took off for UCSB he killed three Asian guys in his apartment. Two of them were his roommates, and one guy was just kinda there, like Steven Wright in the movie Half Baked. This is important to note because Asian lives matter and also because it became a point of contention in subsequent debates on the Internets that hardly had anything to do with the attacks. Third-wave feminists, or as I like to call them, Third Reich feminists, tried to characterize Rodger's rampage as an attack on women, not unlike the ones supposedly taking place in so many dorm rooms, when in fact he killed more guys than girls.

Rodger then left his apartment, with the dead Asian guys, for the Alpha Phi house at UCSB, supposedly home of the hottest girls on campus. I was able to confirm, just now, that the girls of the Alpha Phi chapter at UCSB are in fact hotter than a mofo, via a cursory Google image search. I might investigate further when I get done with this chapter, "for my own personal amusement."

If the girls of Alpha Phi were at home—if they weren't out making some lucky guy's dreams come true—they weren't answering the door. They probably have drills to go over what to do if some creepy-looking guy comes to the door. Even if he's just selling subscriptions to VIBE magazine. Those guys have been known to commit sexual assaults. You never can be too safe. Elliot Rodger knocked on the door several times, to no avail.

Unable to shoot up the hottest sorority at UCSB, Rodger had to settle for a couple of random girls on a sidewalk near the Alpha Phi house—the only two girls he killed that night, I will point out. Turns out these girls were from a sorority called Delta Delta Delta, affectionately known as Tri Delta, not unlike Lambda Lambda Lambda, which as I recall, was a black fraternity in Revenge of the Nerds. The school I went to, Josephine Baker State University, had a sorority that's name was the same Greek letter three times in a row. But I don't think it was Delta. I think it was Sigma. As the saying went, Tri Sig, everyone else has. They looked like they might be easy to have sex with, but for all the wrong reasons.

For the sake of journalism and for no other reason, I also did a Google image search on the Tri Delta chapter at UCSB. Suffice it to say that they weren't quite as hot as the girls from Alpha Phi, though many of them I wouldn't kick out of my bed. Oh, who am I kidding!

The list of people Elliot Rodger shot or somehow injured but didn't kill is longer than you'd think. The wiki has one, natch. After he shot those sorority girls, Rodger jumped into his BMW and took off on a tear through the means streets of Isla Vista, CA, shooting at random people from his car and attempting to run over people on bicycles and skateboards, as if this were GTA San Andreas. He only killed one other guy, by shooting into a deli. Cops nearby saw him drive away, but didn't realize he was the one shooting. Maybe he didn't seem sufficiently mental, according to their assessment.

Eventually, 5-o did give chase. Rodger probably didn't plan for a high speed chase, nor did he practice shooting people from the window of his car. Hence the number of people he shot but didn't kill. I'm surprised he didn't he kill more people with his car. He might have considered focusing more on pedestrians, who aren't as agile, rather than people on bicycles and skateboards. Eventually, he crashed into a parked car, where the cops say they found him with a self-inflicted gunshot wound.

Sometimes I wonder when cops say they found someone with a self-inflicted gunshot wound, especially if it's someone no one would give a shit about if the cops killed them. Notice how people who are wanted for shooting cops are hardly ever captured alive. Elliot Rodger shot it out with a few different cops during his rampage. One of them managed to shoot him in his hip, which might have caused him to crash into that parked car. I can't imagine it helped matters.

It just so happens that, the weekend Elliot Rodger shot up Isla Vista, some shit called #NotAllMen was trending on Twitter. It was a response to girls trying to make it seem as if every single guy, even Mr. Rogers, is a potential rapist. Why would people be discussing things like that on Twitter on a Memorial Day weekend? Because the Internets are a goddamn cesspool.

When feminists found out that a guy attempted to shoot up a sorority because he was upset that he couldn't get any stank on his hanglow, they promptly responded with the hashtag #YesAllWomen, i.e. maybe not all men are potential rapists (Mr. Rogers is dead anyway), but yes all women are at risk of getting shot by guys who don't have any hope of getting their weenies wet, known on the Internets as incels. This kicked off a wave of asinine commentary the likes of which hadn't been seen since the rise of Odd Future.

Come to find out, Elliot Rodger left the Internets with plenty of fodder for everyone's think piece. Before he stabbed those Asian guys in his apartment, he sent off copies of a 200 some-odd page-long manifesto he typed up called My Twisted World. He sent it to his parents, his shrink and a few other people. It somehow found its way to the Internets. His mom might need to check her Facebook privacy settings.

Elliot Rodger wasn't racist per se, but in My Twisted World he laments seeing white chicks with black guys and Asians. He didn't get why a white chick would date a black guy or an Asian when she could date him. He was half-white and half-Asian, and looked like a white guy from the curb. With his odd speech pattern, he could have just told people he was Russian, like that guy Vitaly, who makes those great prank videos.

Chicks fuxwit Russian guys because some Russian guys have a lot of money. Russia's economy is only 1/39th the size of the US economy, which is why the anti-Russia propaganda you hear in the US media is particularly asinine, but they've got a similar problem with wealth distribution. They are the 99%. The guy who really owned the Brooklyn Nets back when Jay Z was pretending to own the Nets is the 1%. Jay Z put up [Dr. Evil voice] one million dollars, and he only owned 1/15th of 1%. Imagine how much that Russian guy spent. I'm not even sure if that would display properly on a calculator. You might get that little e symbol.

YouTube took down the video in which Rodger described his plan to shoot up the hottest sorority at UCSB, which he uploaded shortly before he went and tried to do just that. He may have already killed those Asian guys at that point, I'm not sure. You'd have to find out when exactly those Asian guys died and then check the metadata on the video to find out exactly when it was filmed, and I'm not sure if that's an actual thing that exists or how you would go about doing that. Someone get John McAfee on the phone. YouTube has a policy against videos in which you announce a mass shooting, especially if you're not just bullshitting.

Fortunately, someone saved a copy of the video and just uploaded it on another channel. There's probably like 40 of them, for posterity and also because you can get like $7 every time someone watches one of your videos. You're not supposed to upload videos of people talking about horrible crimes they're about to commit that you stole from someone else's channel, but once you get in the partner program they're actually more lax on policing your content than they would be if you were just some rando. Supposedly, you get about $7 for every 1,000 people who watch one of your videos.

The rest of the videos on Elliot Rodgers channel remained up in the immediate aftermath of his rampage, and they might still be there to this day, for all I know. He'd taken his videos down when he found out his mom saw them, and I don't think he put all of them back up, but there was enough there to fill a solid evening of tragic wonderment.

Rodger was subscribed to The Young Turks, which is run by Cenk Uygur, who had a show on MSNBC for like five minutes before the network had to let him go for criticizing Barack Obama. He was replaced by Al Sharpton, who, like Jay Z, has Obama's personal cell phone number. This became an important talking point in discussions about whether or not Elliot Rodger should be considered a men's rights activist. No true men's rights activist would be subscribed to The Young Turks. Only beta males like No Mames Buey watch The Young Turks.

Tamerlan Tsarnaev, older brother of the dreamy Dzhokhar Tsarnaev a/k/a Jahar, per his YouTube channel, was into Vinnie Paz's solo work and also the Heavy Metal Kings project he did with Ill Bill. Ill Bill is at least Jewish enough that he doesn't respond well to certain kinds of trolling on Twitter, so I'm not sure how halal that was. Maybe he fast forwarded through all of the Ill Bill parts.

Elliot Rodger was a member of a bodybuilding forum despite the fact that he didn't appear to be a bodybuilder. You have to list your height and weight in your profile, so everyone can see how jacked you are and how much progress you've been making in your weightlifting, which is known as "gains." Rodger listed his height and weight at 5'7 135lbs. But people go to bodybuilding forums for reasons other than to share tips on how to work out. Guys on bodybuilding forums are often at the forefront of creeping girls' pics on social media sites like Instagram and Twitter. I heard they're a good place to go to find the top new thots on the Internets.

The same forum Elliot Rodger frequented later became famous when two guys got into an argument about how many days there are in a week. They could more or less agree that there's seven days in a week, but one guy tried to argue that he goes to the gym every other day, which works out to about four to five days a week. The other guy said that if you go to the gym every other day, the most you could possibly go is three and a half days, whatever that means. They argued this to the death. They might still be arguing to this day.

Somehow feminists got it into their minds that because Elliot Rodger was a member of a forum called PUAHate that meant he was a men's rights activist, known affectionately as an MRA. This became its own clusterfuck of bickering over semantics.

PUAHate was a site for guys who can't stand pickup artists, known as PUAs. It was taken offline almost immediately after Elliot Rodger's rampage, which would lead me to believe that there was a lot more illegality going on there than just Elliot Rodger laying out his plans to shoot up a sorority and no one saying shit—which could easily be dismissed as a matter of them thinking he was just foolin'. The server that site was hosted on was probably taken out into a field and beaten to death like the printer in Office Space. Fuck you, PC Load Letter!

Guys on sites like PUAHate, many of whom identify as incels or MGTOW (short for Men Going Their Own Way, a sort of Fleetwood Mac-inspired, libertarian wing of PUAHaterdom), believe there's only two ways you can be successful with women: (1) Have a shedload of money; (2) Be especially attractive and/or good at talking to women. Some guys just have a way with women, the way Cesar Milan a/k/a the Dog Whisperer has a way with dogs. And some guys, like the circa 1992 Billy Ray Cyrus, are so attractive to women that they can have pretty much any woman they want. The only real limit to the amount of women they can impregnate is a matter of time, based on the length of their refractory periods. Eight percent of the guys in Asia are direct descendants of Genghis Khan, the Billy Ray Cyrus of his day.

PUAs teach methods that involve trolling girls in public with canned routines. Some guys recommend picking up girls in nightclubs, while other guys prefer picking up girls during the day in places like coffee shops. Nightclubs are better for scoring with the girl that evening, which I think most guys would prefer. Techniques for picking up girls during the day often involve setting up dates for later that evening or some other evening, when she can be properly plied with alcohol. In addition to getting a girl good and drunk, PUAs teach techniques to toy with a girl's emotions, which makes her more attracted to you; to subtly disorient her, which impairs her decision-making process; and things to do speed along the process of sweet, passionate lovemaking, including things to say if she objects at the last minute, which is just something girls do and doesn't necessarily mean she doesn't want to have sex.

I've read most of the PUA books ever published, because I'm unemployable. The techniques these guys recommend seem like they probably would work if you really did go up to something like 200 girls over the course of an evening and followed their instructions to a T, especially the parts about making sure the girl is good and slizzered and separating her from any friends she may have arrived with. The rest of the rules you can probably adjust or personalize to suit your needs. No two seductions will be the exact same, unless you end up in a situation like Bill Murray in the movie Groundhog Day. Which might actually be ideal, if you think about.

Really, it comes down to a numbers game. In any given nightclub, there's bound to be at least one girl who, like the Asian broad in Can't Hardly Wait, will fuck the next guy who asks nicely, no matter who it is. It could be that she's upset with her father for not showing her enough attention, or it could be that she's trying to get back at a cheating boyfriend, or it could just be that she really likes to fuck; she can't get enough schlong inside her. If a girl like that's gonna be anywhere, it's a damn nightclub. (Another good place to check: the free clinic.) Your mission, should you choose to accept, is to identify this girl. PUAs give you a system to narrow down a group of contestants to one very lucky finalist.

Incels hate PUAs because they can't fathom striking up a conversation with hundreds of women over the course of an evening just to find the one who would be of any use to a guy. They have a hard enough time striking up a conversation with one girl in any five-year span, not counting their mothers. This technique is just not doable. And I don't know if there is another technique. Not another legal technique anyway. Some guys on PUAHate bought books, DVDs, online courses and what have you and felt burned. Other guys didn't even bother. They knew what the technique entailed, and they weren't about to bother. They're jealous of PUAs because PUAs are supposedly out here scoring, and many of them are just as hideous as incels.

It seems that feminists decided Elliot Rodger was a men's rights activist because he was a member of PUAHate, PUAHate has the letters PUA in its name, and PUAs are considered synonymous with men's rights activists, this despite the fact that men's rights activists don't fuxwit PUAs.

Men's rights activists are guys who bitch and moan about men getting taken to the cleaners in a divorce, the fact that marital rape, i.e. sex with your wife when's she's not necessarily interested and/or awake, was declared illegal back in like 1990, the fact that jobs mostly guys work are way more difficult and dangerous than jobs mostly girls work, the fact that some homeless shelters won't take guys, just women and children, the fact that the suicide rate for men is way higher than the suicide rate for women, so on and so forth. They also campaign to have pedophiles freed from prison as if they were Mumia Abu-Ja-mal. Essentially, the men's rights movement is the male equivalent of femi-nism, and in fact it was started by guys who were prominent male feminists.

Typically, a men's rights activist is the kind of guy who already met a woman, married her, had kids by her and got burned by her, whether that was in the form of cuckoldry (often involving a black guy, from what I under-stand), getting thrown in jail for alleged domestic violence, or having child support payments automatically deducted from his paycheck, thus forcing him to retire at the ripe old age of 39 and make ends meet running scams on the Internets, which is known as going Galt, named after a character in Atlas Shrugged. They don't need books of advice on how to pick up women. Also, men's rights activists have female groupies, known as honey badgers. Honey badgers love nothing more than to have sex with men with traditional values. Remember, chicks dig jerks. They show up to men's rights conferences and fuck all the guys.

Basic logic would dictate that Elliot Rodger was neither a PUA nor an MRA. He couldn't have been a PUA because he belonged to a site called PUAHate. That's like being a black guy in the Klan, like Clayton Bigsby. If he'd been an MRA, he could have gone to an MRA conference, given a speech about how he wants to give one of the girls from Jezebel a black eye and scored with a honey badger. Really, it's something he should have considered.

If anything, Elliot Rodger was a male feminist. Why else would he sub-scribe to The Young Turks on YouTube? In his manifesto, he writes of an attempt in his late teens to become a social justice warrior. Acronym: SJW. He may have been under the impression that girls would want to have sex with him because he was an SJW. Male SJWs are often implicated in crimes against women, in part because they're surrounded by the kind of women who are li-able to implicate a ham sandwich in a crime against a woman (lest we forget, a ham sandwich killed Mama Cass Elliot), but also because they buy into the BS feminists spout about how a man is supposed to treat a woman, and they get frustrated when that shit doesn't work. Feminists would much rather bang the kind of guys they pretend to hate on the Internets. That's one of the reasons they write about PUAs so much.

The other reason feminists write about PUAs so much is because it's big business... for somebody. Ironically, many feminists write for sites owned by men. The men who own these sites encourage them to write about PUAs and to try to convince women that they could fall victim to rape and/or a drive-by shooting at any given moment because it fuels outrage, and outrage drives pageviews.

Sites catering to women are particularly profitable because women make the majority of the purchasing decisions in a household, and it's getting harder and harder for guys to find jobs. The way many companies are structured these day, there might be a small handful of guys in charge, and the rest of the people who work there are women. They put a girl in charge of screening employees, and she won't hire very many guys. She definitely won't hire any black guys. Guys end up living in their mom's basement, or with a few other guys. More and more white chicks are having kids out of wedlock, as if they were black chicks.

Corporate SJW sites generate millions of dollars in revenue, of which hardly any trickles down to the girls who write the articles. Most of them make less than what you could make working full time in fast food, if fast food restaurants didn't have sophisticated algorithms to keep you from working more than about 30 hours a week, if you're lucky, so they don't have to pay you certain benefits. The best paid of them make mid-five figures, which is like the blogging equivalent of an A-Rod deal. It's what I one day hope to achieve.

Some of the more enterprising feminist writers at some point figured out that they could supplement their income by pitching articles about PUAs to various publications on a freelance basis. Essentially, what they do is troll PUA websites looking for things a woman might find upsetting. When they hit pay dirt, they fire off an email to an editor, i.e. a girl who's been given a small budget by the guy who owns the site to distribute amongst her friends. The PUAs are more than happy to oblige, because the free publicity helps drive sales of their seduction manuals. They might actually make more from an article intended to throw them under a bus than the girl who wrote it, if not as much as the guy who owns the site she wrote it for.

The feminists can at least take solace in the fact that they're not contributing to any epidemic of violence against women... since I'm sure they know good and well that PUAs don't cause men to commit acts of violence against women, and therefore they don't have to sweat the fact that PUAs' profile has increased considerably as a result of this symbiotic relationship they've culti-vated. They're helping to promote guys they supposedly hate, for the financial benefit of a guy who probably can't stand them either, but they've got bills to pay, and narcissism has led them to believe that they deserve to make a living writing blog posts. Honestly, they probably wouldn't give a shit if a few women did have to be killed. Especially if they were black women. LOL

02.
Burial At Sea

"I need to hear these criticisms, reflect for real, and work on becoming a better person."

— Mahbod Moghadam

Posting Elliot Rodger's manifesto was a no-brainer for Rap Genius, in that it was ostensibly free for them to post and people were bound to be searching for it.

If they could get into the top few results for "Elliot Rodger's manifesto" and related searches having to do with hating women, stabbing Asian guys for stealing your candles and listening to your sister make sweet, passionate love to white guys, who knows how many hits they'd receive.

Mass shootings are always big news for at least a day or two, at a time when only something as big as Charles Ramsey rescuing those girls from his neighbor's basement sex dungeon can trend for more than one day. Even the last few big celebrity deaths didn't last for more than a day.

And Elliot Rodger's Day of Retribution took place on a holiday weekend, which meant that it was bound to be the top story in the news until into the following week. They weren't about to post anything else that weekend. Even if something important did happen, it probably wouldn't have been reported.

Another plane would have had to fall out of the sky... which is something that seems to happen more and more often. CNN is all over those missing plane stories, almost as if they were missing white girls. Could it be that CNN themselves are shooting down those planes? As Donald Sutherland explained in the movie JFK, you look for the one who stands to benefit.

There was minimal concern with Rodger coming back from the dead and issuing a DMCA notice, forcing Rap Genius to remove his manifesto from their site, in part because we don't have the technology to reanimate people who were killed by the police just yet, or else maybe the rioting in Ferguson could have been prevented, and in part because why would he have sent it to the media in the first place, if he didn't want it widely circulated? Duh!

Anyway, you get a few days to respond to those DMCA notices, especially on a holiday weekend. You're supposed to remove any copyrighted material that you're not authorized to post right away, but you can always claim that it took a few days for the thing to arrive in the mail. I happen to know, because I read it on Sandra Rose, that there's no such thing as a legit DMCA notice that arrives via email. That's just someone trolling you, or someone you're not legally obligated to respond to anyway.

If he's really concerned that his grandma briefly appears in a video of his cousin—who later appeared in pron—showing off her cans in a backyard pool, let him send you an actual letter in the mail.

Rap Genius co-founder Mahbod Moghadam spent Memorial Day weekend going over My Twisted World with a fine-tooth comb, looking for opportunities to leave humorous annotations. He'd highlight things that were awkwardly phrased and remark that they were "beautifully written," and he'd use a mention of Rodger's sister to speculate about whether or not she's attractive.

Later, he'd claim that he left these remarks as placeholder text that he'd return to when he had time to clarify and elaborate on his thoughts. At 90,000 words long, per one estimate I saw, My Twisted World is longer than my second book, Infinite Crab Meats, and arguably even more disturbing. I could read it over the course of a weekend, but it would take up a sizable chunk of said weekend, and to leave annotations on it would take even longer. Maybe it wouldn't take Mahbod Moghadam as long, because he went to Yale undergrad and Stanford law, while I went to a glorified directional school, though at the time he was a mere matter of months from having a brain tumor removed. You'd think that might affect his ability to read.

One of the kids they let run Gawker on a holiday weekend saw on Twitter where Moghadam was leaving these ridiculous, insensitive annotations on My Twisted World—which arguably didn't have any business on Rap Genius in the first place—and decided to go in. This was as much of a no-brainer for Gawker as posting Rodger's manifesto was for Rap Genius. Gawker, which is run by gay guys, has had a hard on for Rap Genius ever since the latter got that $15 million from Andreessen Horowitz. They'd already run a shedload of posts on how much of the content on Rap Genius is garbage, the guys who run it are a-holes, so on and so forth. It must be good for pageviews.

It just so happened that Elliot Rodger's Day of Retribution coincided with #YesAllWomen, which was no good for what's known as optics. Women the world over were spending Memorial Day weekend pretending as if what happened in Isla Vista was about them personally, when, lest we forget, Rodger killed more guys than girls (unless you only count Asian guys as three-fifths of a man), and there Mahbod Moghadam was making light of the incident.

Moghadam issued a statement to Gawker apologizing for getting a little bit carried away with his annotations. Rodger's manifesto touched him personally, he said (nullus), because he likes that part of California; it's where he'd like to live one day. He probably figured that would be the end of it. After all, who gets fired on their day off? Only Ice Cube in the movie Friday, and he got caught stealing boxes.

Stealing is the one thing that'll get you fired with a quickness in a shitty service-industry job, no matter what it is and when it took place. Some places won't fire you otherwise. If you commit various other petty offenses, like showing up 15 minutes late every other day of the week, and taking a 45-minute lunch break, they'll just write you up, and once they've written you up enough times, they use it as an excuse to not give you a raise. If you're a bad enough employee, you end up having to wait until the state raises the minimum wage to get a pay increase. I've gotten a raise due to an increase in the minimum wage twice so far in my life, but not necessarily because I'm such a bad employee. The timing just worked out that way. I was a teenager when it went up to $5.15, and then I was back flipping burgers—degree in hand—when it went up to $7.25.

It was announced that Monday, Memorial Day, that Mahbod Moghadam had been fired from Rap Genius. Or asked to resign, if that's different from being fired. I guess being asked to resign looks better, even though it's all over the Internets that this was amidst a scandal having to do with making light of a misogynistic mass shooting, but they might not let you get unemployment if they find out that you quit. Maybe you could explain to someone down at the unemployment office that you had no choice but to quit, or else they might try to sue you or take out a restraining order against you, as if you were Funkmaster Flex. I'd insist on being fired anyway. Quitting is for losers.

Rap Genius may have felt that they didn't have a choice but to post Elliot Rodger's manifesto, to counteract the effects of having been kicked out of Google that past holiday season. The ban actually went into effect on Christmas Day 2K13. Holidays, it seems, are no good for Rap Genius. It might be Allah trying to send them a message.

For years, Rap Genius had been running a scam in which they'd post links to random blogs from the Rap Genius Twitter account, which has a shedload of followers, in exchange for posting links to certain lyrics on Rap Genius. You don't derive any benefit from Google from someone posting a link to your blog on Twitter, but if enough people click on it maybe you can make like a dollar from banner ads. Depending on how much time it takes you to post the links, it might not be such a bad deal.

If all you're doing is copying and pasting some HTML someone already wrote for you, it might not be such a bad way to make money... if there's literally not anything else you can possibly do to make money. It's not altogether different from one of the main things I do other than write these books, posting twerk videos and trying to get a few people to click on them. As amazing as some of those videos are, you don't get much search-engine traffic from them, because the (ahem) models featured in them are obscure to the point where they're probably not even searching for themselves.

Rap Genius used this link-exchange scam to try to boost its search results for albums by the artists people were most likely to be searching for, like Watch the Throne and Justin Bieb(l)er. Lyric searches, if I had to guess, are probably governed by the same power-law distribution as most other things— meaning, in this case, that the vast majority of people search for the same few artists, and hardly anyone searches for anything else.

It's the reason why the aforementioned Watch the Throne album is so thoroughly annotated while, when I checked a while back to confirm that a Freddie Foxxx song called "Swazzee" was the origin of my use of the term cracka-ass cracka, my pet name for white people, I couldn't find it. Sometimes they'll just copy and paste lyrics from OHHLA, the Online Hip-Hop Lyric Archive, and let them sit for years and years without being annotated, which is especially unfortunate in cases of the works of great lyricists like, say, Kool G Rap (and this is supposed to be a community of rap enthusiasts), but they haven't even bothered to post much of Freddie Foxxx's oeuvre.

In late 2K13, Mahbod Moghadam wrote to an obscure tech blogger to try to get him to post links to Justin Bieb(l)er lyrics on Rap Genius in exchange for posting a link to his blog from the Rap Genius Twitter. It didn't make sense why a tech blog would post links to lyrics to Justin Bieb(l)er songs, and later I couldn't help but wonder if Moghadam contacted this guy on purpose, to try to throw Rap Genius under a bus.

A lot of those tech guys hate Rap Genius, because they're envious of that $15 million. These are guys who sit around in their moms' basements fantasizing about the day when their own hot tech startups issue an IPO, at which point they can fly well-known Instagram thots out to the Bay Area for sweet, passionate lovemaking, which is what a lot of those tech guys do. I've had guys contact me offering exorbitant amounts of money to put them in touch with random hoo-ers I posted on my blog. Of course I didn't take them up on it, because that would be disrespectful to women and also because you can never be sure that it's not just law enforcement trying to entrap a brother.

An exec with Google was supposedly murdered by a hoo-er he found on one of those Seeking Arrangement websites that connect rich guys with girls who claim they're trying to pay their way through college, but it may have just been an accidental heroin overdose. Why would a girl kill a guy who's paying her an allowance each month? You want to keep a guy like that alive for as long as possible. I'd try to get in touch with whoever's defending her in court, but I can't be messing around with IV drug users.

This tech blogger/wannabe startup guy posted about Rap Genius' SEO scam on a popular tech message board. There a guy from Google saw it and announced he was looking into it. Rap Genius was fucked. Having Google's top anti-spam guy announce that they're looking into something you're doing that's obviously just gaming the system is like having 5-0 go on the evening news and announce that they plan to review video of you selling crack to schoolchildren—you're as good as caught.

I was on my first mimosa of the day, on Christmas, when my phone started blowing up with people hitting me up to let me know that Rap Genius had been kicked out of Google, which in effect meant that they'd been removed from the Internets, since the vast majority of people who visit Rap Genius come from Google. No one visits Rap Genius for the BS annotations.

I spend Christmas at my cousin's house in North St. Louis. If you've ever seen that scene in the movie National Lampoon's Vacation where they get off the highway in St. Louis to ask for directions and a buncha black guys steal the hubcaps from the Family Truckster, that scene was actually filmed on her block. It looks even worse now than it did back in 1983. I spend the entire day there getting my drink on, and by the time I get done I'm not at all concerned with any danger I might be in walking to my car at night in that area.

This year, I had even more reason to celebrate. People were hitting me up because they knew that I'd famously been involved in a beef with Rap Genius in which I came into possession of transcripts of racist discussions that took place in Rap Genius' private editors chat room, a good six months-plus before the Snowden affair, and Mahbod Moghadam threatened to kill me. And now not only had Rap Genius effectively been destroyed, but on Christmas Day no less.

Rap Genius wasn't banned from Google so much as it was buried deep within Google. A search for Rap Genius didn't turn up anything other than articles about how Rap Genius had been banned from Google. The site itself was way down on page 50. The vast majority of people who search for something on Google click the first link that comes up that isn't some sketchy ad, which oftentimes is the wiki. The links on the first page are governed by a power-law distribution not unlike the lyrics in Rap Genius, with that first link being a Justin Bieb(l)er album and the last few links being Freddie Foxxx's post-Industry Shakedown output (much of which isn't half bad), and hardly anyone clicks on the second page. It's possible that no one had visited the 50th page of Google until it was necessary to do so to find out how deep Rap Genius had been buried.

To paraphrase Tom Venables, Rap Genius had been buried so deep within Google, whoever could pull it out would be crowned King Arthur.

Without a high ranking in Google, traffic to Rap Genius plummeted.

People hadn't been clicking on Rap Genius because they gave a shit what some rando had to say about a certain bit of text; they were clicking on it because it was the first result for any number of names of songs and random phrases. Now that it wasn't, they'd just click on something else. They weren't about to click through 50 pages of god knows what to find Rap Genius. And since Rap Genius' ridonkulous valuation wasn't really based on anything other than the fact that it was one of the most high-traffic sites on the entire Internets, it was essentially ruined.

Alas, it was only a matter of time before Rap Genius was back in Google's good graces. It was probably just a matter of Marc Andreessen, the guy who gave Rap Genius that $15 million, calling over and pulling a few strings. Google is just as much of a scam as Rap Genius, if not worse, because they're this vast conglomerate that runs seemingly the entire Internets. Not only do they control what you can actually find when you search for something, they're tracking every single thing you do on the Internets, much of which you probably do using one of their services, and using it to sell you something, or selling it to another company that uses it to sell you something, who knows.

Google could give a rat's ass about someone finding out how to game the system; they just don't want people thinking they'd allow someone to game the system. Hence publicly announcing that they were looking into Rap Genius and then issuing the death blow on Christmas Day. In fact, they've been known to turn a blind eye to companies that spend a lot of money on those ads that turn up at the top of a list of search results. At one point, JC Penney ranked highly for seemingly any consumer product you can possibly buy from JC Penney and probably even shit they don't sell. They got caught and hit with a fake penalty, not unlike Rap Genius. They were back on top a few months later.

All Rap Genius had to do to pull themselves from the depths of Google and hence be crowned King Arthur was email the sites they'd paid to post their links and ask to have those links removed. They built some sort of tool to automate at least part of the process, as they explained in a widely-heralded mea culpa. They were commended for their honesty, just for admitting that they did something wrong after they'd already been caught and punished. As if. Stories about the bravery they showed may have been planted in tech publications owned by Andreessen Horowitz, from which they then spread.

In the end, Rap Genius may have actually benefited from getting kicked out of Google, because of the amount of publicity generated and the number of articles written about it, many of which included links to Rap Genius. If there weren't as many of them as there were links from the link-exchange scam, which they had to get rid of, they were from higher-ranking sites, and Rap Genius may have gotten more of a boost from them than they got from links from some loser's blog.

Rather than an isolated incident, Mahbod Moghadam's annotations on My Twisted World were merely the latest in a string of incidents in which he generated bad publicity for Rap Genius, and that may have been why they didn't waste any time getting rid of him.

In 2K13, he surreptitiously took a picture of Mark Zuckerberg, Ben Horowitz and Nas having dinner at Zuckerberg's house, after being told not to. Ironically, Zuckerberg, who's built a vast fortune on harvesting people's personal information, can't stand to be photographed. The aforementioned Gawker used to troll him by posting stalkerazzi pictures of his wife, who has powerful cankles despite being Asian. Moghadam deleted the pic from his Instagram and issued a formal apology to Zuckerberg, probably on orders from Ben Horowitz, but not before legendary bored-hoodrat blog The YBF got their hands on it. The version of the pic they posted still circulates the Internets to this day and was used to illustrate many a blog post about how Moghadam later ordered Zuckerberg to suck his dick.

Moghadam was a guest on a podcast by a guy who runs a tech email newsletter. The conversation somehow turned to Mark Zuckerberg, whom Moghadam described as being similar to Dustin Hoffman's character in the movie Rain Man. In Rain Man, Hoffman refuses to go outside when it rains, insists on being home in time to catch The People's Court, and throws a fit when Tom Cruise tries to force him to get on a plane—to go to Las Vegas to count cards, natch. Moghadam claimed that Zuckerberg only feels safe in his house, and that's why they had to meet there.

In addition to ordering Zuckerberg to suck his dick, he said that the New York Times is "Carlos Slim's ho." Born with a perfect name for a pimp, Carlos Slim is a Mexican telecom billionaire and one of the richest people in the world. He once expressed an interest in buying the New York Times, and he might even have a stake in the paper, but don't quote me on that. The New York Times had run a story critical of Rap Genius, in the wake of my beef with the site in late 2K12. Around that same time, I started working on my second book, Infinite Crab Meats, which has a chapter on Rap Genius. It was released in early 2K13, around the time when Moghadam met with Zuckerberg et al. and took that picture.

Later that year, Moghadam threatened to rape then SPIN editor Christopher Weingarten in his mouth. Weingarten had pointed out on Twitter than the annotations for the song "Put Cha Dick in Her Mouth" by Three-Six Mafia were particularly asinine... if you can imagine. Three-Six Mafia is the group that won an Oscar for the song "It's Hard out Here for a Pimp," from Hustle & Flow, one of my old man's favorite movies. "Put Cha Dick in Her Mouth" is one of their classics from the pre-Hustle & Flow era. With lines like "I'mma get my chief on while she suck my ding dong / Eyes like a ching chong, hard on like King Kong," there's basically no way that the annotations for "Put Cha Dick in Her Mouth" wouldn't have been asinine. It's the Rap Genius equivalent of the episode of Beavis & Butt-head where Buzzcut told them they weren't allowed to laugh or else they'd be kicked out and have to go to Hope High School, where they'd get their asses kicked on the reg, and then promptly began yelling about peens, vagines and masturbation. It was hopeless.

Mahbod Moghadam, running the Rap Genius Twitter account, saw Weingarten's tweet about the "Put Cha Dick in Her Mouth" annotations and responded that he was going to rape Weingarten in his mouth. The media picked up on this and quickly let loose with any number of blog posts about how one of the founders of a venture capital-funded startup is out here threatening to rape people in their mouths (but at least it was a guy).

Moghadam copped a plea, claiming that many people had the password to the Rap Genius Twitter account, and it must have been one of them who threatened to mouth-rape Christopher Weingarten. It was obviously a lie, but of course you lie when you're the founder of a company that's received $15 million in venture-capital funding and you get caught threatening to rape someone. Probably at least a few people did have access to the Rap Genius

Twitter account, and as long as Twitter doesn't have a way to determine whose actual fingers are typing something—which I'm sure they will eventually—that probably would have been enough to get by in court. Lest we forget, Mahbod Moghadam was once a lawyer.

Rap Genius then pulled one of the top new moves in Internets fuckery, later used to devastating effect by Iggy Azalea. First they issued an apology via the Rap Genius Twitter account, and then when seemingly half the sites on the Internets posted that they'd apologized, they deleted both the apology and the tweet with the rape threat in it so that it was like it never happened.

Note that Rap Genius never apologized, nor were they called to apologize by the media, when they compared the most dark-skinted member of Das Racist to a burnt cigarette, when they joked about raping black women during slavery and when they threatened to kill me.

A few weeks after Moghadam was let go, it was announced that Cleveland Cavaliers owner Dan Gilbert was investing $50 million in Rap Genius. This was in addition to the $15 million they'd already received from Andreessen Horowitz, plus whatever else they'd received both before and after that that wasn't as widely reported. Who knows how much they've received altogether, those fuckers.

The deal was announced in a story on the site Business Insider that featured embedded Rap Genius annotations. Embedded annotations were supposed to be one of the innovations designed to expand the scope of the content they covered and to make them less reliant on Google, to prevent what happened that past Christmas from happening again (like in a Wham! song) and to justify that $50 million from Dan Gilbert.

Andreessen Horowitz co-founder Marc Andreessen has a stake in Business Insider, so this arrangement was beneficial both in the sense that it was guaranteed that Business Insider wouldn't print anything that could potentially harm Rap Genius and in the sense that it increased the value of his investments in both the site running the article and the site the article was about. For all we know, he probably had investments in other random shit that was advertised on the page. He was getting paid six ways to Sunday.

In the story, it was announced that Rap Genius was changing its name to just Genius, in an attempt to shed its past image and negative publicity and expand into different markets. The domain name was changed to genius.com, which rapgenius.com now redirects to and for which they probably had to pay a shedload of money, rather than having content about technology, the law, politics and what have you hosted on what was ostensibly a rap music website. Imagine trying to quote something you found on Rap Genius in court. They'd bury your ass underneath the jail. Whoever could get you out would be crowned King Arthur.

The two remaining co-founders also posed for new press photos that seemed to have more of an indie-rock vibe than the slightly-disheveled hype-beast look they were going for in the past. The overall impression that you got was that they'd exploited hip-hop as much as they could or felt was necessary and now they were on to bigger and better things, probably as they'd planned all along.

In the article, Tom Lehman and Ilan Zechory distance themselves from the SEO scheme, which Lehman—the tech guy—probably invented. Zechory says he was off in Detroit courting Dan Gilbert, so there's no way he could have been involved. Do they even have the Internets in Detroit? If they do, it's arguably a matter of misplaced priorities.

The article's title says that Mahbod Moghadam was fired, though Moghadam himself, on Facebook, insisted to me that he resigned. If that were the case, why would he allow Business Insider to run an article that says he was fired. People might read it and think he was fired. Not only is the title, "How Rap Genius Fired a Co-Founder and Scored an Investment," or something to that effect, in the article itself Lehman and Zechory discuss "firing" Moghadam. Again, lest we forget, Mahbod Moghadam was once a lawyer.

On Twitter, someone asked Ben Horowitz if he forced Lehman and Zechory to fire Moghadam. He said it was their decision, which I took to mean he told them that Moghadam had to go, and they decided to fire him rather than, say, have him killed. They didn't have to fire him, if they didn't want to— they had options!

My theory is that Lehman and Zechory wanted to issue another BS apology and then delete both the apology and the offensive remarks after the fact, and maybe force Moghadam to have a seat for a while, like Malcolm X after he

compared the Kennedy assassination to chickens coming home to roost, but
Ben Horowitz was like fuck that shit. Moghadam had to go.

Moghadam and Horowitz's relationship has been at least somewhat hostile
ever since. Horowitz criticized an article Moghadam wrote for the infamous
Thought Catalog about how to steal from Whole Foods, and they ended up
going back and forth on Twitter. The tone of Horowitz's subsequent comments about Moghadam called to mind Michael Corleone lamenting the fact
that Fredo chose to side with someone else over his own family, like maybe he
really did consider having Moghadam rubbed out and now he was regretting
that he didn't.

It's possible that Moghadam cost Rap Genius—and hence Horowitz—a
shedload of money. The deal with Dan Gilbert had yet to be finalized when
the Elliot Rodger thing went down, and it was temporarily rescinded until the
heat from that could blow over. The amount of the deal wasn't announced
until it was completed. Could it have been for even more money, if it wasn't
for the Elliot Rodger thing, not to mention getting kicked out of Google, which
Moghadam has been blamed for (whether or not it was his idea in the first
place)?

Also, it may have been felt that Moghadam didn't serve a purpose, now that
they'd landed a whale. He didn't do anything for the site other than generate
publicity, much of it negative, and now they didn't need as much publicity.
Zechory was the one who landed the deal. He went to Detroit and spotted
Dan Gilbert's handicapped son in the audience of a Pistons game. He was
easy to spot because he has a giant head, like Brain from Pinky and the Brain.
Zechory, a licensed hypnotherapist, pretended to befriend the poor bastard
and talked him into introducing him to his father.

Nick Gilbert has some sort of weird cancer that causes his brain to sprout
benign tumors. That's why his head's so big. Eventually, it might get to the
point where he can't balance it on his shoulders without it tipping over, and
they have to build some sort of support structure. There may have been concern that Moghadam is rumored to have only pretended to have a brain tumor
as an excuse for having told Mark Zuckerberg to suck his dick. People with
brain tumors, like Vietnam vets, can tell when someone's faking it.

03.
Perpendicular To The Swooshtika

"Billionaires prefer black women; they are loyal and guard your interests."

— Ben Horowitz

Andreessen Horowitz co-founder Ben Horowitz's father David Horowitz, the legendary racist, was a sort of auxiliary member of the Black Panthers back in the early '70s.

An editor of the leftist magazine Ramparts, which published—among other things—many of the letters from prison that later became Eldridge Cleaver's bizarre, fascinating Soul on Ice, and the article on the JFK assassination that Oliver Stone's JFK is sorta kinda based on, he assisted the Panthers in raising money for charity initiatives, from rich white people, that the Panthers probably then spent on cocaine, which was a lot more expensive back then than it is now. It used to be known as a drug for rich white people only, and part of the Panthers' revolution involved making it affordable for black people, namely themselves.

Horowitz helped purchase a building and fill out the paperwork for a school that was funded in part by federal grants and in part by a mafia-style protection racket, which the Panthers also used to fund their famous free breakfast program. If only they still had a free breakfast program, for adults.

Horowitz had a girl he knew from Ramparts take a look at the school's finances, and she ended up getting kidnapped, bludgeoned to death and dumped in San Francisco Harbor, where her body washed up a few weeks later, supposedly on orders from Huey P. Newton, who by then had already fled to Cuba to escape prosecution for killing a 17-year-old prostitute.

There was an excellent article on Newton's flight to Cuba, aided by Bert Schneider, the guy who produced Easy Rider, a while back in an issue of Playboy, which I read for the articles. Cinematic in nature, I'd describe it as a sort of depraved, black radical variation on the movie Argo, which itself was based on article in Wired magazine.

Later, Horowitz would allege that when Huey P. Newton kicked Bobby Seale out of the Panthers, possibly because of an argument about a potential Black Panthers film produced by the aforementioned Bert Schneider, Newton fucked Seale in the ass so hard he had to be taken to have his asshole repaired by a surgeon who was sympathetic to the Panthers' cause. Though he made it clear that this was just punishment; it wasn't a sexual thing.

Between the bufuing and what happened to the white chick, Horowitz felt it best to distance himself from the Panthers and make himself scarce for a period of time, only to reemerge in the mid '80s with a famous article about why he's not a leftist anymore. Since then, he's turned his attention towards trolling campus liberals and declaring his opposition to reparations for slavery, interests he combined by trying to take out ads in college newspapers for his list of reasons why reparations for slavery are a bad idea, one of which, he says, is the fact that black people were sold into slavery by black Africans and dark-skinted Arabs, so why should white people have to pay reparations?

For his efforts, he's been declared a racist by no less an authority than the Southern Poverty Law Center. It should be pointed out though that the SPLC is not the same organization that it was back when it was represented by Jack Nicholson's character in Easy Rider. Back then, it had ostensibly pure motives and worthwhile objectives. Today, the SPLC is known for putting random, self-styled Internets pickup artists—guys who, for all we know, might not even be slaying that much pussy—on lists of hate groups alongside the Klan. Also, I recently read an article in New York magazine that I think made a pretty good case that the Internets' current problem with political correctness is a direct result of the ridonkulous political correctness on college campuses—as depicted in the film PCU—that Horowitz the elder was railing against back in the late '80s, early '90s.

Horowitz the younger is married to a black chick and has three Halfrican American children. I'm sure it's awkward, to say the least, to have a black wife and a white father who's officially racist. Imagine what family dinners must be like, if they have family dinners (it doesn't say in the wiki). Not only would I be concerned that the conversation might turn to, like, anything other than the weather, but it's a known fact that racist white guys loave lurve luff black women.

A lifelong hip-hop head, Ben Horowitz is known in tech circles for starting posts on his blog—filled with BS LinkedIn-style advice on how you too can be a tech billionaire, clearly intended to appeal to the terminally unemployed—with quotes by rappers like Nas, Kanye West and Young Jeezy. It may have been his idea to invest in Rap Genius and also to bring in Nas as a sort of paid black public cosigner. Nas, who's had problems with the IRS and the State of Georgia for years now, as immortalized by Jay Z in a line on The Blueprint 2: The Gift & the Curse, was given a small stake in the company in exchange for becoming Rap Genius' first verified artist and pretending to be friends with Ben Horowitz at tech conferences.

Horowitz also has a pet rapper, some ex-con he found on Twitter who calls himself Divine, not to be confused with RZA's brother, the drug dealer, and any number of Five Percenters. Is this guy a Five Percenter? Having read an article on Ben Horowitz and his love of rap music in the New York Times, Divine trolled Horowitz on Twitter until he got a follow back, and then submitted theme music for an Andreessen Horowitz podcast, at which point he was named the official Andreessen Horowitz rapper.

Divine and Horowitz have since posed for a picture in matching outfits. In it, Horowitz looks like Divine threatened him with forcible sodomy just before it was taken. If his father is aware of this, I'm sure he's deeply concerned.

Perhaps it's fitting, given Ben Horowitz's taste for brown sugar, that Rap Genius' business model is at least somewhat akin to slavery.

In slavery, white men purchased black people at auctions, including one at the present day location of Wall Street, which is just precious. They purposely selected for guys who looked like they could do tough, grueling labor without randomly dropping dead, which was an especially bad problem on the sugar plantations in South America and the Caribbean, and guys who looked like they'd be especially prolific breeders. Hence the NBA and the NFL. They

looked for girls they'd like to have sex with and also girls who looked like they'd
be loyal and guard massa's interests. If possible, all of the above. Sometimes
it was necessary to break up families, though as many a blowhard is quick to
point out, more black kids were living in two-parent households during slavery
than in 2015.

At Rap Genius, white kids copy and paste rap lyrics from OHHLA and
then use them to dominate search results for said rap lyrics and probably all
kids of shit that doesn't have anything to do with rap music. Sometimes they
talk rappers into coming up to the Rap Genius offices and typing up their
own lyrics, especially obscure rappers and newer artists, whose lyrics aren't
in OHHLA, plying them with a big black garbage bag of marijuana, which
they first purchased with that initial $15 million investment from Andreessen
Horowitz.

They prefer it if rappers type their own lyrics into Rap Genius, because if
they do, they can't turn around and sue, but what kind of rapper's gonna spend
the time it takes to type up his own lyrics? Even for free weed! Chief Keef
couldn't even recognize his own lyrics on the page. That shit could have been
the lyrics to "Bohemian Rapsody," for all he knew.

For all the lofty talk about Rap Genius as a "knowledge project" and the Internets equivalent of the Talmud, whatever that is (it might be that scroll Ryan
Gosling had in The Believer), its true value lies in the amount of search-engine
traffic it receives. It's one of the most high-traffic sites on the entire Internets,
and there's probably not a site that does that kind of traffic that wouldn't be
worth boatloads of money. Even those pron tube sites, which also are amongst
the most high-traffic sites on the Internets (admittedly, thanks in part to yours
truly). Otherwise, how could they afford the sheer amount of bandwidth it
takes to serve those Lord of C*mshots compilations for hours and hours on
end? Shout out to the guy who puts those together, who of course reads my
blog. Of course it could just be a vast money-laundering operation for someone
making mad money off the books from drugs or some other illegal activity: they
pretend to make hundreds of millions of dollars from the Facebook of Sex,
whatever that is, they pay taxes on it, and whatever's left over is perfectly legit
money, at least as far as the government knows.

Rap Genius once toyed around with the idea of charging law firms an annual fee for access to crowdsourced annotations of legal texts. The plan was to charge much less than whatever Lexis-Nexis was charging, Undercutters Pizza style. That must not have worked out for them. If they never can figure out a good way to actually make money, they can probably still make boatloads of money from plastering the site with shitty banner ads, the same way a pron tube site does, if not enough to justify the ridonkulous amount of venture capital they've received. Remember, they're not paying a damn thing for the content, so any money they receive from ads would be pretty much pure profit.

Legally, you can't just post someone else's intellectual property on the Internets and profit from it to the tune of tens of millions of dollars, or else I wouldn't be writing these books. I'd be too busy cashing checks from material I copied and pasted from someone else's books. Or trying to, anyway. But when the major labels objected to Rap Genius posting the lyrics to songs they owned the rights to, Rap Genius simply cut them in on the deal. The few major labels still left at this point were all given a small percentage of Rap Genius similar to the stake Bono had in Facebook.

When Facebook went public, Bono became an instant billionaire and probably the richest rock star, ahead of Paul McCartney, who had to give a significant amount of his fortune to a girl with one leg, which is wrong on so many levels. If Bono were to wake up with Jay Z's money, he'd jump out of a window. He really does care that much about money, or else he'd just give his Facebook stock to Africa. It's not like he needs it. He's been rich since like 1980. He must think we're dumb.

Similarly, if Spotify ever goes public—if it doesn't go out of business first, because it loses money hand over fist year in and year out and has no clear path to profitability—the major labels stand to reap substantial windfalls. Way more than Rap Genius got from Andreessen Horowitz. And for what, just letting some kids posts song lyrics on a blog? They didn't even have to type up the lyrics! The artists, meanwhile, probably aren't getting a damn thing. I mean, if the labels own the rights to the songs, and the labels sold off the rights to said songs to Rap Genius. The artists don't enter into it.

David Lowery, the guy from Cracker and Camper Van Beethoven, of "Take the Skinheads Bowling" fame (it was in Bowling for Columbine), made a big stink about Rap Genius—and a number of other lyric sites—posting song lyrics without a signed permission slip, revenge pr0n style. A study was conducted, and it was suggested that a lawsuit might be necessary. Lowery teaches music business, or something along those lines, at Georgia Tech, and he's been one of the foremost opponents of seemingly any music-industry business model other than the classic 20th century record deal, complete with a baggie of coke and a few hoo-ers in the limo. It's likely that he isn't in any position to sue even if he wanted to, given that he was signed to a major label during the post-Nirvana alt-rock sweepstakes, when the TIs were cutting checks for [Dr. Evil voice] a million dollars to any dumbass in a flannel shirt. He probably signed over his rights to benefit from things like Rap Genius and Spotify.

As is the case with Rap Genius, the true value of Spotify lies in the number of subscribers it has, and to a lesser degree, the number of bums who are willing to subject themselves to a commercial every half hour or so in order to use it for free. Therefore, it's in their best interest to try to drive the number of people who use Spotify, no matter what it takes. The only reason they're not sending girls to your house to blow you in exchange for using Spotify is because it would probably still cost more than they stand to make on a per-user basis. But it's only a matter of time until that's not the case anymore, the way things are going. In the meantime, they're just gonna have to settle for letting boatloads of people use Spotify for free in exchange for listening to the occasional ad that probably doesn't even make them very much money, and giving people access to Spotify Premium, i.e. the full-featured pay version, for free or for some tiny fraction of what it should cost, for a few months, at which point you can just cancel. If you're like me, you might not have a choice in the matter. Who's got $10 a month these days?

When Taylor Swift pulled her music from Spotify, it was because she didn't want it included in that free tier. You don't make much money from people who actually pay for Spotify streaming your music—er, at least compared to what you'd make if they actually bought your album on CD—but you don't make shit when people who use Spotify for free stream you music. You're basically giving it away for free, when you could just as easily be charging for it. A pimp would never stand for some shit like that. The TIs could give a rat's ass about not making as much money from non-paying users, because they want Spotify to have as many users as possible, for when it experiences a "liquidity event." Taylor Swift can do whatever she wants with her music, because she's got one of those hybrid deals, like Macklemore—the TIs don't own her music, they just distribute it for a fee. It's the kind of deal black artists would get, if they had the sense god gave geese. When Taylor Swift pulled her music from Spotify, it was presented in the media as a publicity stunt to promote her album, as well as an attempt to make as much money as she possibly could from it. 1989 sold 1.3 million copies its first week out—in 2k14, mind you—and thus became the year's best-selling album.

What Rap Genius does is not altogether different from what the Huffington Post does. All the top tech companies are built on exploitation. They're like the pron industry in that sense, except less interesting to me personally.

The Huffington Post copies and pastes the most important information from articles published on other websites and then uses SEO to dominate search results for that information. Technically, what they do isn't plagiarism, because they don't copy and paste the entire article—just the part anyone would want to read—and they do provide attribution.

It's not uncommon for HuffPo to publish its own knockoff version of someone's article, days after the fact, and have their knockoff version dominate Google. HuffPo also dominates Google for things like the time when the Super Bowl begins and celebrity sideboob, one of the main things people search the Internets for other than song lyrics. HuffPo has its own separate subsite, known as a vertical, dedicated to celebrity sideboob.

HuffPo was co-founded by Arianna Huffington, Jonah Peretti, and Andrew Breitbart, all of whom seem to have undergone a Horowitz the Elder-style ideological conversion at some point in time or another.

Huffington, the lady the site's named after, was once a conservative. She was married to one of those Republican guys who are obviously down-low homosexuals. He came out of the closet after he lost a Senate race back in the mid '90s. That was the end of their relationship, obviously, but she kept his last name and then named her website after it because her own name is Greek and probably just looks like transcribed gibberish.

Breitbart, the legendary conservative troll, was a researcher for Arianna Huffington back when she was also a conservative. That's something to keep in mind the next time you're tempted to take her seriously. I've taken this to mean that Andrew Breitbart used to write her articles, because I'm a sexist. (I'm right though.)

Many big-name journalists, including Fareed Zakaria, pay random kids to write their articles for them. In The Last Magazine, a thinly-veiled account of his time at Newsweek, the late great Michael Hastings breaks down how this process works. Essentially, Zakaria gives some kid a list of talking points, the kid writes the article, Zakaria gives it a once over and it's published. He's since been caught red handed plagiarizing and was forced to cop a plea by explaining that he doesn't actually write his own articles.

The Last Magazine, written in the late '00s, was published posthumously a couple years ago, after Hastings crashed his Mercedes into a tree, at which point it exploded. He may have been assassinated by the Illuminati. Before he died, he warned his colleagues that he was being investigated by the CIA and that he had a big scoop. He'd already gotten one of the most high-ranking members of the military fired for some shit he said about Obama off the record.

It's considered politically incorrect to suggest that a woman doesn't write her own work. Bjork complained about this in an interview with Pitchfork, which is a couple of years now into a tragically misguided experiment in appealing to Third Reich feminists. Fortunately, a lot of their money comes from festivals rather than the website. The fact of the matter is that Bjork, back when she was about something, worked with a number of male producers. It says so right there in the CD booklets.

Breitbart is also known for having been Matt Drudge's weed carrier back in the late '90s. He found some of the links that were posted on the legendary Drudge Report—arguably the ur blog—and later started his own site that was frequently linked to by the Drudge Report, oddly enough, and could be viewed as a sort of proto Huffington Post.

Interestingly, Breitbart claims to have been raised a typical Hollywood liberal in LA's Brentwood neighborhood, where OJ used to live, and was only radicalized by Clarence Thomas' Supreme Court confirmation hearing—which really was some ol' bullshit. Anita Hill, who went out on a date with Thomas after the pube-on-the-Coke-can incident, purposely tried to throw him under a bus because she thought he might vote to repeal Roe v. Wade.

In the years following his work with HuffPo, Breitbart was instrumental in getting Shirley Sherrod fired from the Department of Agriculture, posting a video that had been edited to make it seem like she was explaining why it's important to hate white people, when in fact she way saying the exact opposite.

He may have still had an axe to grind with black women from the Clarence Thomas confirmation hearings, and that's another reason why it's important for women not to issue false sexual harassment allegations: it could lead to "blowback," not unlike how our meddling in the Middle East in the '70s and '80s may have led to 9/11.

In 2012, Breitbart got into an argument with author Chris Faraone about Occupy Wall Street. As I recall, Breitbart was convinced that girls were getting raped in those tents. It just goes to show the extent to which his thought process was dominated by identity politics and sex crimes. Andrew Breitbart was the white Kanye.

This put the kind of people who would actually show up to Occupy Wall Street in the weird position of having to either side with Breitbart or accuse girls of lying about rape. It was the most brilliant thing he ever came up with.

Perhaps he understood, on a certain level, that his work here was done. The next day, Andrew Breitbart dropped dead in someone's driveway, walking home from a bar where he'd had a glass of wine. Later, it was announced that he'd died of "natural causes" at the ripe old age of 43. Faraone went on to release a book called I Killed Breitbart.

Jonah Peretti was once a '90s-era anti-globalization activist of the No Logo variety. I remember once seeing him on the Today Show in college, where he discussed a controversy having to do with his attempt to get Nike to print the word sweatshop on a shoe.

Nike used to have this program—I think they still have it—where you can pay extra to have your name printed on a shoe, along the side of the shoe, sort of perpendicular to the Swooshtika (TM). He tried to get them to print the word sweatshop, as a tribute to where Nikes are made. They wouldn't. A lengthy email exchange ensued. It later went viral on the Internets, one of the early examples of the phenomenon.

Ironically, Peretti evolved over the course of his adulthood from being against sweatshops to running the Internets equivalent of a sweatshop.

HuffPo was built on, on the one hand, aggregation, and on the other hand, blog posts written for free, for "exposure." When HuffPo sold to Aol for $315 million, they didn't give the kids who wrote those blog posts a damn thing. Not even so much as a pizza party. I got more free shit from Kmart in the years immediately following their emergence from Chapter 11 bankruptcy—and not because I was stealing, thank you very much.

Using what he learned about virality from the Nike sweatshop incident and what he learned about exploitation from the Huffington Post, Jonah Peretti went on to found BuzzFeed.

BuzzFeed started out with a widget they invited people to place on their blogs. The widget would identify things that were about to trend on the Internets, and then BuzzFeed would create their own knockoff version and reap the traffic windfall. It may have also collected information about the people who visited those blogs, which they could somehow sell to advertisers, which is essentially what sites like Facebook and LinkedIn do.

In exchange for posting the BuzzFeed widget on your blog, BuzzFeed would occasionally post links to your blog, not unlike the scam Rap Genius ran to rank highly for Justin Bieb(l)er Lyrics. Of course when BuzzFeed started to blow up, they got rid of the widgets and stopped linking to the kids who'd supplied a lot of their early content.

BuzzFeed also paid kids to copy articles from other sites more or less verbatim, changing a word here and there so that they wouldn't be identified as the exact same articles by Google, which won't rank an article as highly if it appears to be redundant.

Once BuzzFeed received venture capital funding and attempted to become a legit news site, hiring a guy from Politico to cover the 2K12 presidential election, they had people go through and delete all the plagiarized stuff en masse.

One guy must not have gotten the memo and continued right on plagiarizing content, not just from (ostensibly) legit media outlets like the New York Times and National Review but Wikipedia and Yahoo! Answers.

Perhaps sensing the hypocrisy of firing a kid for plagiarism on a site built on plagiarism, Jonah Peretti jumped to the kid's defense and issued corrections for the few plagiarized articles that had been identified at that point. The few black people who were aware of this scandal followed along intently, to get a sense of what it must be like for your boss to look for reasons not to fire you.

More plagiarized articles were identified, prompting a review of the kid's entire archive, and come to find out, he'd committed plagiarism on the reg. That's pretty much all he did. Only then did Peretti fire the kid and cop a plea, explaining that BuzzFeed didn't start out as a legit news organization.

The kid, who'd worked for Mitt Romney in '08, then took a job working for National Review, one of the sites from which he'd plagiarized, in a development that may have constituted Peak Caucasity. Essentially, he got fired for stealing and was then given a job by the people he stole from.

Now that BuzzFeed is attempting to be a legit news organization, they pay a few kids to write feature articles and articles on politics. This content is read by relatively few people and is only there to make the site seem legit.

Aside from soliciting investments from venture capitalists, BuzzFeed makes most of its money from articles written by advertisers that are designed to be indistinguishable from regular editorial content.

BuzzFeed pays Facebook a fee to promote its content. That's why there's always something from BuzzFeed in your newsfeed even if you haven't "liked" BuzzFeed. In return, Facebook cuts on the traffic fire hose. BuzzFeed receives a shedload of referral traffic from Facebook.

BuzzFeed cites its huge amount of traffic, most of which it just buys from Facebook, to advertisers. BuzzFeed then has one of its writers work with the advertiser to come up with a post sponsored by the advertiser's product. BuzzFeed doesn't pay Facebook to promote these posts, and sometimes hardly anyone reads them.

It used to be, brands could run an ad on some shitty network sitcom and be seen by like a hundred million people, back when there were only like 230 million people in the US. Now no one watches sitcoms, just people in jail and a few old people who haven't died yet. Media outlets like Vice and BuzzFeed have convinced brands that they can reach millennials, and that's why they're supposedly worth billions of dollars.

The whole thing is a joke, and when the bottom finally falls out, it could be the thing that causes our society to descend into a state of full-on chaos.

In August 2K14, about a month to the day after it was announced that Rap Genius received $40 million from Dan Gilbert, it was announced that

BuzzFeed received $50 million from Andreessen Horowitz, at an $850 million valuation. According to math I did just now on the back of an envelope, Andreessen Horowitz purchased about 6% of the company for that amount.

A year before, Jeff Bezos from Amazon purchased the Washington Post, i.e. a huge, legendary newspaper, for $250 million.

Supposedly, before BuzzFeed got that $50 million from Andreessen Horowitz, they were trying to sell the entire company to Disney for $1 billion, but Disney was like fuck that shit. A few random dumbasses on the Internets argued that this would have been a good deal for Disney. They may have been working for Marc Andreessen in a sock-puppet capacity.

Marc Andreessen is not above using Bond villain tactics, and in fact he kinda looks like a Bond villain. His head is shaped like an egg. Nick Gilbert arguably has a better-shaped head. Andreessen supported Mitt Romney in the 2K12 presidential election, which meant that every time you clicked on Rap Genius, in a roundabout way, you were helping sell black people back into slavery.

At a private fundraiser for a group of millionaire donors, Romney was caught on tape explaining that 47% of the people in this country don't pay taxes and therefore he's not at all concerned with their well-being. There was no way these remarks could have been deceptively edited by Andrew Breitbart, because he'd already been dead for a couple of months at that point.

It's since been announced that Marc Andreessen is working on robots designed to replace people in low-paying service industry jobs. If he's actively trying to get rid of people's jobs, and the candidates he supports advocate cutting off services to people who can't work for a living and hence don't pay taxes, what are those people supposed to do?

That must be what the FEMA camps are for.

Dan Gilbert made his fortune from Quicken Loans, a website where you can get instant approval for a home loan with no money down. Applicants are encouraged to overstate their income, and the amount of the loan is based on a BS estimate that might be three times the actual value of the property.

If it's just a website, how can they be sure it's not an eight-year-old applying for a loan? If they actually gave you the money in cash rather than cutting a check to a bank or mortgage company, which I'm sure is what they do, you could flip that on some cocaine and probably become a millionaire. You could be the next Big Meech, who, incidentally, is from Detroit.

Once the loan is originated, it's sold off to the kind of companies that brought the global economy to the brink of collapse in '08, where it's combined other shitty loans and sold as an exciting investment opportunity to the senile elderly and local governments in backwater towns in Alabama. The towns go bankrupt and have to fire all but two cops, who are no longer allowed to respond to domestic violence calls. Domestic violence skyrockets. The elderly are at least fortunate that they're already almost dead, and if they can't get their prescription meds, they might not have much time left anyway.

Gilbert uses his Quicken Loans money to build casinos and to bribe local governments in desperate Midwestern cities like Cleveland and Detroit to legalize gambling.

His casinos prey on precisely the kind of people who would finance a house with a loan from a website that would give a home loan to a child. They gamble for enough money to pay back their mortgages, and of course they lose. Even if they win, they're just gonna use that money to pay back their loans.

If they lose, they get foreclosed on, and the empty house drives down the property value for the rest of the houses on the block, leading other people to abandon their houses. Dan Gilbert then buys those houses for pennies on the dollar.

Dan Gilbert owns 8 million square-feet of real estate in downtown Detroit alone.

Meanwhile, people in Detroit can't afford water. In the summer of 2K14, right around the same time Gilbert was dropping $40 million on Rap Genius (and Eric Garner was getting choked out by NYPD), Detroit threatened to shut off water to as many as half its residents, if they didn't pay past due water bills.

Utilities are notorious for setting multiple final dates for shutoffs. A date was set for people's water to be shut off if they didn't pay their past-due bills. They didn't, probably because they honestly didn't have the money, and the city didn't do anything, suggesting they'd been bluffing all along.

How many employees does the city even have to go around and shut people's water off? What would happen to the tank, if they closed half the city's faucets all at once? The idea that some shit like this would even be an issue, in one of the richest countries in the world, in what used to be one of the richest cities in the world, represented a new all-time low. This seems like the kind of thing that would happen in some third world dictatorship.

I was in college when a company named Bechtel attempted to privatize the water in Bolivia. They jacked up the prices for water and wouldn't even allow people to collect rain water in a Styrofoam cup and drink it, like kids in the ghetto do, because technically that water belonged to the water company.

Protests erupted, and eventually martial law was enacted. Under martial law, the military is allowed to shoot civilians on sight without providing a warning, let alone a justification. One kid got shot in the face. At that point, the government told the water company they were on their own, and the guys from the water company were forced to haul ass before people found out where they were.

It was announced that Detroit might have to auction off $5 billion worth of art kept in the Detroit Institute of Art, from back when Detroit was one of the richest cities in the world.

This plan seemed even more farfetched than the idea of cutting off water to half the city if people didn't pay their bills by a certain date. Who's even looking to buy $5 billion worth of art from Detroit? They probably couldn't get a very good price for it. Everyone knows they're desperate.

It may have just been a PSYOP to condition people to think that there really is no money in the city, when one guy there owns like half of downtown.

04.
The Lovable Old James

"You simply don't deserve this kind of cowardly betrayal."
— Dan Gilbert

There's something decidedly antebellum about the fact that Dan Gilbert lets his son represent the Cleveland Cavaliers in the NBA draft.

I don't watch very many basketball games, let alone the NBA draft, but from what I understand, they make a big spectacle of the white guys who own the teams selecting which black guys will play for them next season and therefore make millions of dollars and (temporarily) leave the ghetto.

All the black guys wear ridiculous-looking suits like Steve Harvey wears on the new Family Feud. There may or may not be a transparent bubble, shaped not unlike Nick Gilbert's head, with ping pong balls in it, like when they used to announce lottery numbers on the nightly news. Is that how they decide which team gets to pick first?

At any rate, they've allowed Nick Gilbert to be involved in the process. There's less risk of him not picking someone sufficiently athletic, like at a slave auction, because they're all athletic, by definition, and also because the team probably already decided who they're going to pick. He's just there for the formalities.

Allowing a team owner's special-needs son to point out the player he'd like to pick in the draft is roughly the equivalent of your boss letting his son follow you around as you mop floors for a living, pointing out spots you missed, or sit in an interview and decide if you get the job, based on his own personal eight-year-old whim.

Am I reading too much into this?

Lebron James' return to Cleveland was announced in a big fancy article in Sports Illustrated that broke the Internets as if it were pictures of Kim Kardashian's huge naked ass—as if we haven't seen video of Ray J balls deep inside of her. It just goes to show how fragile the Internets are.

The article, its announcement and what have you, were purposely designed to make it seem as if returning to Cleveland were a matter of principle, but you'd have to be someone who watches both sports and news shows about sports on the reg to believe this was about anything other than the almighty dollar.

Regardless of his salary, Lebron will make more money long term returning to Cleveland, because it's better for his brand. He'll be able to charge more to shill for various consumer products, which is where all of the real money is.

If he'd stayed in Miami the rest of his career, or went wherever someone was willing to cut him the biggest check, he'd look like someone who's only motivated by money, and ironically, he wouldn't have been able to make as much money.

Going to Miami in the first place made him look like someone who couldn't carry a team to a championship on his own, and the fact that they couldn't win three rings in a row seems kinda pathetic, given that they had such a stacked roster. If only he'd known they wouldn't be able to threepeat he could have left after that second win.

Aside from the weather and the girls from Ass Parade who probably hang out there when they're not filming, the only reason he went down there in the first place was to ensure that he'd win a few rings, for branding purposes. Sticking around in Cleveland his entire career, he ran the risk of becoming the next Charles Barkley, maybe the best player of his generation who never won a ring. Charles Barkley probably has boatloads of money and has been allowed to work as a commentator for decades now despite the fact that he's an idiot, but if he had a ring he'd probably have even more money!

Charles Barkley once got caught getting a blowski in the car, N.O.R.E.-style, and I remember it sounded to me like the girl might have been a pro. (If she was a civilian, I'd say she was definitely a keeper.) Charles Barkley is still on TV. Warren Sapp got caught copping a blowski at like 7 AM the morning after the Super Bowl, and he was out of a job by the time I was done with my breakfast—and I don't think he has any money from when he used to pay football. He might still receive that same pension OJ receives, if it's not possible to sell that off. I remember he sold off his Super Bowl rings.

Imagine the psychology of someone who collects Super Bowl rings from broke players. What if it turned out it was one of the team owners buying those rings? I wouldn't be surprised.

Now that Lebron is back in Cleveland, it doesn't matter if he can't win another ring. He's already got two, so they can't say that he's never won, or that he only won once. If he never wins again, it'll just be viewed as a matter of the team not being good enough. Even Jordan had to have Scottie Pippen before the Bulls started winning. Pause.

It's likely Lebron chose to announce his return to Cleveland in Sports Illustrated because he announced The Decision on ESPN, the other big name in sports media, and he didn't want anything about this next move to remind people of the widely-criticized Decision.

The article seemed every bit as stage managed as the announcement of Gilbert's investment in Rap Genius, in Business Insider, aside from the fact that neither Gilbert nor Lebron has a stake in Sports Illustrated. If athletes are allowed to either buy or start their own media organizations—which could be viewed as a conflict on interest—they don't seem interested. A few former players have stakes in teams, but I don't know of anyone who has their own magazine or cable network. If they did, the players could give that guy all the exclusives and tell ESPN to suck it.

Any time you see an individual arrange for a certain media outlet to get the big exclusive on a story, you kinda have to assume that the information in that story is at least a little bit suspect, if not completely inaccurate. Never ever buy an album from an artist who has a big feature in Pitchfork the week their album comes out, and then the album receives like an 8.4, which is still good enough to merit a Best New Music designation, and then later it's announced that they're one of the headliners at that year's Pitchfork Music Festival, or next year's, depending on what time of year the album is released. That shit is all coordinated between the artist's PR firm and the business department over at Pitchfork. The album might still be good, if it's an artist who consistently drops hot shit (no Danny Thomas), but it could be terrible.

The article in SI reads as if either Lebron put it together himself based on a list of talking points provided by a publicist or they had someone attempt to write it in Lebron's voice and then he gave it a once over to make sure they didn't use any words he wouldn't normally use, anything conspicuously lengthy. There does seem to be something suspiciously simplistic about the prose. Professional athletes, in interviews and what have you, tend to use overly complicated words and sentences. Like the shit Mike Tyson used to say, but without the lisp.

"My style is impetuous, my defense is impregnable, and I'm just ferocious."

The content of the article was BS. Any sentimental attachment to Northeast Ohio he claims to have is rendered moot by the fact that he ditched Northeast Ohio in the first place, and in such ridiculous fashion. Imagine writing a letter to a girl you're trying to get back with and telling her you love her despite the fact that you kicked her from a moving vehicle, Gucci Mane-style, and haven't seen her in three years. She'd never believe you. Even girls who'd date Gucci Mane wouldn't believe that. Love means never having to say you're sorry for kicking someone from a moving vehicle.

The worst part about both the article in Sports Illustrated and Lebron James' return to Cleveland was the fact that he was crawling back to the guy who'd been so disrespectful to him. Those of us who mop floors for a living sometimes don't have a choice but to work for racist white people, but Lebron James has millions of dollars.

When Lebron announced that he was leaving Cleveland for Miami, Dan Gilbert responded with a letter in which he went off on Lebron, posted on the Cavs' website. It was the kind of letter you only write to someone you plan on not seeing again in life, and it was the kind of letter only the owner of the team would have been allowed to write. Dan Gilbert didn't have to worry about his boss censoring it or punishing him for writing it, because he was the boss. Rappers wish they had that kind of creative freedom.

He basically called Lebron a piece of shit and wished him nothing but pain and bad health. He declared that the Cavs would win a championship before Miami ever did, almost as if the fix was in. It made me wonder if he really would pay to have the Cavs win the championship. The thing is, maybe you can buy a win if you can make it to the championship, but I don't know if you can buy your way all the way through the playoffs. I don't have a problem believing that sports are fixed. In fact, I suspect that the 2K15 Super Bowl was fixed, because they didn't want Marshawn Lynch to be viewed as a hero after his little performance at the Super Bowl press conference.

Ironically, the letter was written in comic sans, the same font used for many I Can't Breathe t-shirts, to protest the death of Eric Garner, who was choked to death by the NYPD for no apparent reason. Years later, Lebron would wear a comic sans I Can't Breathe t-shirt before a Cavs game. White racist NBA fans on Twitter were none too pleased.

Jay Z supposedly provided I Can't Breathe shirts (not in comic sans) to Brooklyn Nets players to wear on the court before the same game, at the Barclays Center, right across the street from Jay's old stash spot as mentioned in "Empite State of Mind." dream hampton, who co-wrote Jay's book Decoded, announced on Twitter that it was Jay Z who arranged for the shirts to be delivered to the Nets players. She was the same one who revealed that Nas used ghostwriters on his dreaded n-word album, after someone on Twitter asked her why Jay can't get political.

Note that I don't necessarily mean to suggest that Jay (supposedly) bringing those shirts was a publicity stunt. I'm sure his motives were pure.

The ridiculous font of the letter was in stark contrast to its content. Tonally, Gilbert all but called Lebron a dreaded n-word. Shit, I've been called a dreaded n-word by (white) people who weren't as disrespectful. Gilbert didn't suggest that Lebron shouldn't be allowed to play for whatever team he wanted to play for, provided he was no longer contractually obligated to play for Cleveland, but clearly that's how he felt.

———

If there's a precedent for the magnanimity (if you will) Lebron showed in going back to Cleveland, it was that time Michael Jordan refused to endorse a black candidate in an election in North Carolina over a virulently racist white candidate. Republicans buy Nikes too, Jordan famously argued. It was disgusting!

Jordan may have honestly been able to tip the election, with an endorsement and maybe a donation. Jordan was that famous, the race was close enough, and it's not like Jordan didn't have the money. Jordan didn't get paid much from the Bulls until towards the end of his career, and I suspect—without knowing anything about the business of basketball—that he was never paid what he was worth, but he was in literally a million commercials going back to the late '80s.

Anyway, the guy was a virulent racist. How do you not endorse someone running against a virulent racist in an election? You could fuck around and get sold back into slavery. Jordan is just lucky that black people love expensive tennis shoes enough to look past his shortcomings, so to speak. His "brand" could have been damaged.

Lebron returning to Cleveland just so happened to coincide with Jordan becoming the first ex-NBA player to become a billionaire. Jordan owns a majority stake in the Charlotte Hornets, and the value of the team recently increased to the point where Jordan is now, at least on paper, a billionaire—this according to Forbes magazines, which probably just pulls numbers out of its ass.

Jordan first bought a minority stake in the team back when BET founder Bob Johnson was majority owner. Johnson had been the richest black person in America, and the first black billionaire, until his wife took him to the cleaners in a divorce. Now Oprah Winfrey is the richest black person in America.

I suspect that one of the reasons black men have such a hard time getting ahead in this country is that we're held back, on a subconscious level, by the knowledge that the richest black person in America isn't even a guy. I'm not saying that a woman shouldn't have the most money, if she did the most work and provided the most value. I'm just saying. Lord knows black men could use a few positive role models. If one of us can't get it together, maybe someone can rob Oprah.

Now Michael Jordan is both the first NBA player and the only black person to have a majority stake in an NBA team. The wiki says he owns more or less all of the Hornets, without saying who owns the rest. It might be the Illuminati. I wouldn't be surprised if they insist of owning a minority stake in each NBA team for whatever reason. Even Dan Gilbert is listed as the majority owner—rather than the owner outright—of the Cavaliers. Whereas it took Jordan decades to stack a billion dollars, I can't imagine Gilbert needed someone to go in with him on that purchase.

Michael Jordan is maybe the best NBA player of all time (I only hesitate to say because what do I know?), but he never would have made a billion dollars, and enough to become the only ex-player majority owner, just from playing basketball. The only way a black man can make that much money is by aiding white people in ripping off vast numbers of black people. You gotta be the black public cosigner in a sketchy business deal, like when Jay Z was brought on as part-owner of the Nets to (emotionally) appease people who were being gentrified out of Brooklyn.

I look around, and I see so many people wearing Air Jordans, even umpteen years after the fact, I think about what they cost, and I wonder if Jordan shouldn't have way more than a billion dollars. Keep in mind, that billion he has is from the Hornets, the money he made as a player, hot dog ads he did in 1992 and all kinds of shit. The amount he made from the shoes might be some small fraction of that. Similarly, it was revealed that Jay Z only ever owned one-fifteenth of one percent of the Nets. Of course that was after the stadium was built and operational and he was ready to give up his stake in the team.

I guess it doesn't matter if you're getting paid what you're owed in any given deal, when you've got like a million deals.

———————

There was a time when black people really weren't allowed to leave the team they played for, so to speak, let alone own it.

In the years before the Civil War, slaves in Kentucky could escape to Lebron James' native, beloved Ohio, a free state, by walking across the Ohio River during the winter, if the weather got cold enough that the river froze solid. If it didn't, and you tried to walk across it anyway, you were screwed.

Leonardo DiCaprio in the movie Titanic, in a tragic bit of foreshadowing, described falling into a freezing body of water in the Midwest as akin to being stabbed by a thousand knives. It might even be worse than slavery.

Some slaves attempted this anyway, because that's how fucked the fuck up slavery was. Imagine if you were a slave, and in order to be free all you had to do was walk across a river that appeared to be more or less frozen. You'd at least have to seriously consider it.

A woman named Margaret "Peggy" Garner, perhaps an ancestor of the guy who got choked out on Staten Island, crossed the Ohio River along with her husband, an infant child, a few other kids and several other people. Some of them escaped to Canada on the Underground Railroad, which I was disappointed to find out—in the third grade—wasn't really a train.

Garner stayed with family in Ohio, not far from where they crossed into the state, while an uncle attempted to make arrangements for them to escape elsewhere, where they were less likely to get caught. You don't want to escape into a free state and then settle somewhere near where you escaped from. I wouldn't want to live too close to the river even if I were free. I've seen 12 Years a Slave.

Black people in Ohio, back during slavery, lived in certain enclaves for free blacks. Oftentimes there weren't a lot of people who lived in those areas, so inbreeding was rampant. I'm sure they would have been happy to see a few new faces. To this day, a lot of black people who live in certain parts of Ohio are all related.

Somehow the Garner family ended up getting caught. A house negro probably ratted them out while they were hiding beneath the floor like the Jewish family in the beginning of Inglourious Basterds.

US Marshals, ordered to search every field house and outhouse in the area, surrounded the house Peggy Garner was in and pulled "akickdoe." In order to prevent her kids from being returned to slavery, she stabbed one of them and would have stabbed the rest of them and also herself, if they hadn't gotten to her in time. She wasn't right in the head.

Legally, they couldn't try her for murder without sending her back to the plantation in Kentucky and then having her extradited to Ohio to stand trial. They were all about justice, and they were also all about holding black people in captivity.

Back in Kentucky, massa put her on a boat to Arkansas, which—little known fact—you can reach by boat from Kentucky, to work for his brother, rather than having someone from Ohio come and throw her in prison, where she wouldn't have been of much use to anyone other than perhaps the people who lived in the town where the prison was located, who would receive federal funds based on the number of people in the prison, in addition to the number of people who actually lived in the town. This was before private prisons you can invest in, from which anyone who owns stock can benefit.

On the boat to Arkansas, either crazy-ass Garner tossed her infant child overboard, or the boat was hit by another boat and the child was accidentally thrown overboard during the collision. At any rate, Garner was said to have been happy that the child drowned and hence wouldn't be raised in slavery.

Garner's story was the inspiration for the Pulitzer Prize-winning novel Beloved, which was later adapted into a film starring Oprah Winfrey, the richest black person in America, male or female.

05.
We Banned
For Life

*"When you pay a woman for sex, you are not together
with her. You're paying her for a few moments to use her
body for sex. Is it clear? Is it clear?"*

— Donald Sterling

Donald Sterling, owner of the LA Clippers, loved black-ish pussy—but he didn't want to be seen as someone who loved black-ish pussy.

He didn't want his jumpoff, V Stiviano, inviting black guys to Clippers games and posing for pictures with them on Instagram. Someone might see those pictures and get the impression that she's the kind of girl who makes sweet, passionate love to black guys two at a time, like in film, allowing them to use her as a pair of Chinese handcuffs.

V Stiviano is half-black and half-Mexican. She pointed this out in one of the recordings of her conversations with Sterling. Sterling must have been aware of this from jump but felt that she could "pass"—if not as a white chick, then as a full-on Latina, rather than a half-black chick. She doesn't have such a dark complexion, but she has the kind of swarthy, ethnically ambiguous facial features that you see in a lot of Instagram models. She could play an Asian chick in a Hollywood film, in a pinch.

Later, it was revealed that V Stiviano may have been one of Bishop Don "Magic" Juan's hoes. Or rather, there was a picture of her kicking it with the good bishop on his Instagram, and he seemed to want to give the impression that she was one of his employees, so to speak. He suggested that he gave her advice on how to separate Donald Sterling from some of his billions of dollars, and presumably she brought it back to him to spend on pimp cups and fancy green and gold outfits. (The green is for the money, and the gold is for the honeys.)

Bishop Don "Magic" Juan was a real pimp in Chicago back in the '70s, according to one of those pimp documentaries that used to come on HBO back in the late '90s. His hoes used to walk a stroll near the basketball stadium where the Chicago Bulls play, not far from where the Pitchfork Music Festival is held (which seems strangely appropriate). At some point, he gave up pimping to become a preacher, the ultimate in pimpin', and later served as spiritual adviser to Snoop Dogg, not unlike how Jesse Jackson served as Bill Clinton's spiritual adviser in the wake of the Monica Lewinsky scandal, before it came out that he had "outside kids."

Talk about the blind leading the blind.

––––––––––––

The way the NBA works is, team owners make more or less the same amount of money regardless of whether or not their team is any good. The only real incentive to try to win a championship, or a lot of games, is because you actually give a shit about sports, and you'd feel different if your team won than if they didn't win. You might not make any more money, and you could actually lose money.

The bulk of a team owner's income, from what I understand, based on something I saw on Real Sports with Bryant Gumbel (which I watch religiously despite not being that into sports) a long time ago, comes from TV income. The NBA collects all of the money it receives from networks for allowing them to show games on TV and splits it up evenly among the team owners. It's probably necessary for them to do this, or else the few teams that seem to always be on TV—like the Miami Heat and the LA Lakers—would make all of the money.

Sometimes I'll end up watching a basketball game at my cousin's house on Christmas. The room with the TV in it is one of the better places to sit and pound drink after drink if for no reason other than having the day off from work. It's where I was when I found out Rap Genius had been temporarily removed from the Internets. There's some extremely vulgar kid who must be the boyfriend of some distant female relative of mine or someone's friend who was invited over. He gets extremely "turnt up" during Lakers games. I can't remember if he likes the Lakers or if he dislikes them. Maybe he just likes shouting profanities. At any rate, they always seem to be playing on Christmas. The NBA probably makes a lot of money from that game. Even my dumb ass is watching. And you can't just record a game and watch it later and fast forward through the commercials. You gotta know exactly what happens when it happens, because that shit is important!

Only one team can win the championship each year, and it seems like the same teams keep winning over and over again. Even if you give a shit which team wins, I'm not sure if attempting to be especially successful is the best way to maximize the value of your investment. Donald Sterling increases the profitability of the Clippers by doing more or less the exact opposite. He doesn't purposely try to lose. What he does is, he spends as little on the team as he possibly can and hopes for the best. If they still somehow manage to win, so be it. He'll make even more money. But they'll have to do so with a shitty roster of players. Er, a roster of players that he's paying as little as he possibly can. He avoids signing players who cost a lot of money, and if one of the kids he found for a discount gets good enough to demand a high salary, he just trades them to another team for someone in his price range, i.e. towards the low end of whatever the going rate is. Since Donald Sterling bought the team, the Clippers have lost more games than any team in the NBA.

The Clippers have been one hell of an investment for Donald Sterling. He bought the team in 1981, the year I was born, for $12.5 million—probably a shedload of money by 1981 standards, more like $30 or $40 million today, but still way less than you can buy an NBA team for. If teams still cost that little, the players would be able to buy their own teams, and the whole system would be ruined. Alas, the league has since increased in value by orders of magnitude. Sterling got in right before the league got hot, with guys like Magic Johnson, Larry Bird and Michael Jordan. Nullus. It was the equivalent of investing in Apple Computer in the early '80s, right around the same time Sterling bought the Clippers, on a hot tip from a heroin addict, like Forrest Gump. If teams that were only worth $12 million are now worth billions of dollars, largely due to guys like Michael Jordan, how come Jordan barely has a billion dollars, according to some BS article in Forbes? I'm glad you asked that question. It shows you've been paying attention.

Donald Sterling has similarly, erm, unorthodox strategies for increasing the value of his investments in real estate. He's been in real estate since the '60s. That's how he got the money to buy the Clippers. He owns a lot of rental properties and apartment buildings in LA. He prefers not to rent to black people, Mexicans, people with children and people on Section 8, and he's developed strategies to avoid renting to those groups and to drive them out of places he buys where they already live.

If he buys a building where blacks, Hispanics and the like already live, he drives them out by refusing to accept their rent checks and then citing them for nonpayment.

Admittedly, I'd be wary of taking a check from someone who lives in a Section 8 unit or a not particularly nice apartment building. Not that I advocate housing discrimination against minorities and the less fortunate. I'm just saying. People who live in shitty areas tend to not having checking accounts—hence the Rush Card—and how can you write a check if you don't have a checking account?

I spent my 20s paying my rent in sweaty handfuls of twenty dollar bills, the same way some of the girls I follow on Instagram are paid for a day's work. I'd actually bring it down to the headquarters of the real estate company that owned the building I was living in, which was between where I was living at the time and where I grew up. (Of course it was.) I've had a checking account and the same book of checks since the week I started college, but I've never felt confident about writing a check for anything that costs more than delivery pizza. That's just asking to have your account shut down and be taken advantage of by Russell Simmons. I'm not trying to be the next Kimora Lee.

If you can write a check for the entire amount of your rent—one that will clear—there's no reason why you can't just go down to the bank and get cash for the same amount. I can see plenty of reasons why you wouldn't want to, e.g. the time it takes to get money from the bank, having to stand in line behind the elderly, and take it elsewhere, the risk of getting "got" with that much cash on you, so on and so forth. But I could almost see why Sterling would insist on cash... I mean, if I didn't know that he was purposely trying to drive certain groups from his rental properties.

Another thing he'd do is refuse to make repairs and then show up for a "surprise" inspection. He'd know when to show up for the inspection because his least-desirable tenants would tip him off when they demanded something be repaired. He's crafty like that.

Every landlord does this, at least to a certain degree, because you don't make money in real estate from fixing a place up to the point where it's a nice place to live—especially if it wasn't particularly nice when you rented it out. You want it to be just nice enough that your tenants can't get someone from the city to come down there and declare it condemned or have you arrested on one of those BS slumlord and/or absentee landlord laws that were passed in response to the release of the Joe Pesci film The Super.

With Section 8 properties, in particular, there's a certain minimum standard of comfort and safety that you have to reach in order to be accepted into the program in the first place, because the government is the one paying the rent, rather than the unscrupulous hoodrat living there, and the government's not about to pay for just any old thing. Or rather, they're not about to pay you for just any old thing. Your name is (probably) not Halliburton. My house is shitty enough to be a Section 8 property, just in terms of floor plan, amenities and what have you, but it's likely I'd have to spend thousands of dollars to get it to the point where they'd accept it. I might have to spend more than it's worth.

Sterling is accused of killing an old black lady, whose apartment he refused to fix. Both her shower and her toilet stopped working, and then she had a stroke, and it's alleged that the stress brought on by Sterling refusing to fix her shower and toilet may have caused her to have the stroke. She may have been taking a shit in the tub after the toilet stopped working. Sociologist Alice Goffman describes a family using a bathtub as a makeshift outhouse in her book On the Run, about young black guys caught up in the criminal "justice" system.

Sterling may have been hoping that the old black lady's living situation would deteriorate to the point where she'd just move out. I don't know why he didn't just pull one of his surprise inspections and then have her evicted. Maybe he was busy banging one of his hoo-ers. The older he gets, the less he can get done in the course of any given day. It's hard enough moving houses when you're 26 years old. An old person is liable to just sit there and fester until they drop dead. You hear stories all the time about old people being found dead in their apartments, where they've been sitting for two years... situations where no one thought to conduct a wellness check.

Donald Sterling is a firm believer in stereotypes, which is why he loves Asian people. He prefers to hire Asians in the various companies he runs because they bow their heads, apologize and promise to do better whenever they make a mistake—or rather, when they're accused of making a mistake—whereas black or white people (he probably doesn't employ very many black people in a non-basketball player capacity) would probably get upset with him for pointing out something they did wrong. And he prefers Asian tenants in the buildings he owns because they'll accept an apartment in whatever condition it's in and they won't issue a complaint no matter what. If they're handy with tools, like Mr. Miyagi in The Karate Kid, they might even fix things themselves and make various improvements to the property.

Generally speaking, Asians don't have a problem living in a place that's a little bit run down. Hence the state of most Chinese restaurants. They buy those places from white people, who took a certain pride in the cleanliness and the style of the décor, and then they just proceed to sling as much rice as they possibly can, until someone from the city gets a look at the back area and forces them out, to be replaced by some garbage chain establishment. If it's in a hood area, they might just continue on indefinitely, because who gives a shit? Chipotle doesn't want to open a location there anyway.

Another reason you see so many Chinese restaurants in hood areas is because black people love Chinese food, because it's delicious.

Donald Sterling is kinda like Charlie Sheen in that he doesn't pay girls to fuck, he pays them to leave, except he probably also has to pay girls to fuck. Charlie Sheen, if he's got his teeth in, and his hair plugs straightened out, and if he's had a bath recently, could probably still pull girls on the basis of his looks. He's getting on in years, but girls prefer a guy who's got a few miles on him. Men of a certain age look distinguished, whereas girls after a certain point look gross.

Donald Sterling has to pay twice every time he has sex, but it's no big deal, because he has boatloads of money. If Donald Sterling woke up with the amount of money Charlie Sheen made for doing that show Anger Management on FX—after he got kicked off Two and a Half Men for going on the Alex Jones show talking about how he was bi-winning—he'd jump out of a window. And Charlie Sheen made like $200 million from that show. He really was bi-winning. He'll never have a problem scoring.

Donald Sterling forces his jumpoffs to bring him AIDS tests, as if they were pr0n chicks, to prove to him that he can raw dog them and still safely have sex with his wife. It might be the most baller thing anyone ever did ever, for a number of reasons, including the following:

1) Most guys would feel awkward trying to talk a girl into getting tested for AIDS, let alone getting tested for AIDS on a regular basis as a condition of having sex with a guy in his '80s—and that's why most guys don't own billion-dollar real estate and sports empires. You gotta have balls to be the king.

2) Sterling's wife was aware of the fact that he was banging hoo-ers on the reg, and in fact, the AIDS tests may have been her idea. While I'm not sure why he'd want to continue banging some old hag—maybe he was afraid she'd divorce him and take half the Clippers—how many guys could talk their wives into allowing them to bang hoo-ers on the reg? Imagine the two of you opening that envelope from the free clinic each month, maybe turning it into a special occasion, opening a nice bottle of wine and lighting a candle. You gotta have control over a woman's mind to pull some shit like that. That's that Bill Clinton-level pimping.

Sterling's expert mind manipulation wasn't just limited to his wife. He had techniques for dealing with his hoo-ers. Rather than just putting them on an allowance, like girls from those Seeking Arrangement dating sites who fuck old men supposedly to put themselves through college, Sterling pays his hoo-ers by the sex act. And he only cuts them a check periodically, based on a running tally he keeps in his head, like West Indian Archie in the movie Malcolm X. He could write down each act in a notebook, along with the girl's name and a system of tally marks, but the police might find it, and technically it's illegal to pay a girl to have sex with you.

In the case of a girl who sued Sterling in '03, he was paying her $500 per act, presumably regardless of what the act was, and she was said to want it constantly, either because his pipe game was that vicious or because she was trying to get as much money as she possibly could. Maybe she was saving up to buy a house. The fact that he's older than dirt would suggest to me that it was the latter. At any rate, the idea of a girl who wants to make sweet, passionate love to you at all times, whom you have to purposely try to avoid, if you want to get any work done, is even more appealing than the idea of having enough money to be able to score whenever you feel like it, which I'm sure would also be fantastic. If you've got the means, you'd much rather just pay a girl by the act rather than cut her a check for the same amount each month, provided you could talk her into it.

One of his hoo-ers he actually had to sue just to get her to move out of his house. She hated the idea of having to give up that $500 per throw, but it was time for him to trade up to a newer model. 1993 was such a good year for rap music; maybe girls who were born that year are especially good in the sack. There's only one way to find out. Because it's a known fact—both in his household and amongst his friends and people he deals with professionally—that Sterling likes to get worked on by a professional, and because he's at minimal risk of going broke from paying for sex, it was nothing for Sterling to take this case to court. The resulting trial, and a few other times he's been sued, are the source of much of what we know about how he, erm, manages his affairs. It's not like he'd just tell you. That game is to be sold, not told.

It's been a known fact that Donald Sterling is a racist, filthy old hoo-er monger and a terrible team owner since at least as far back as some point in the 2000s, when I saw it on an episode of HBO's Real Sports, and probably further back than that, but it wasn't until V Stiviano leaked audio of him getting on her for hanging out with black guys that it occurred to people that it might be necessary to take his team from him.

Before then, it was said to be impossible to get rid of a team owner. You can't just take away someone's property because they're racist and they like to pay for sex, let alone something that's worth billions of dollars, it was thought. Otherwise, what company wouldn't be at risk of being taken over? In retrospect, this may have just been an excuse not to act, as long as Donald Sterling's, uh, proclivities weren't a significant PR problem for the league.

When Sterling's fellow team owners and various commentators said it was impossible to get rid of an owner, what they really meant was that there wasn't anything any of them would do to rob a fellow owner of his privilege, because what if it turned out that Donald Sterling wasn't the only owner who hated black people and liked to buy pussy? This could be a slippery slope!

In fact, as Sterling soon found out, it's probably easier to get rid of a team owner in the NBA than it is to get rid of the owner of any other kind of company. Alas. The league commissioner, in this case Adam Silver, a younger guy personally selected as David Stern's replacement, can unilaterally ban an owner from the league—which means that he'd be gone from the league "for all intensive purposes," aside from still owning the team. And then, per league bylaws, a three-fourths vote of team owners—not unlike the votes necessary to free black people from slavery in the first place—can force an owner to sell his team.

Of course Sterling's fellow team owners didn't like the idea of having to force out one of their own, but once it got to the point where a vote was taken, you didn't want to be the one guy siding with a racist hoo-er monger with a thing for girls who seem like they might be kinda black. Imagine how awkward that would be, if they ever had to meet with their players. That's why it was important when Latrell Sprewell choked the shit out of his coach: it made it clear that just because these players are being paid millions of dollars, and therefore it would be a terrible idea to do anything that would put that in jeopardy, doesn't mean they won't randomly choke the shit out of you. The moment white men no longer fear that a black guy might randomly choke the shit out of them is the moment when black men are truly at risk.

Of course that didn't prevent some people from trying to argue that Sterling was given a raw deal. Both Mark Cuban and Bill Maher, who's become increasingly suspect in his old age, argue that it was unfair to punish someone for things they said in a private phone conversation recorded unbeknownst to them. Boo FN hoo!

Actually, I sorta kinda agree, in that once the precedent is set, you know good and well they're just gonna use it to throw black guys under a bus. You can kinda assume that anything you say on the phone now, and probably anything you say in the presence of a phone, regardless of whether or not you're using it, is being recorded, in addition to anything you say in an email or post on the Internets.

Imagine if the NSA had that level of technology back when Bill Cosby was out there doing his thing. Not only would his career be over, he wouldn't have made hundreds of millions of dollars in the first place. They would have caught him slipping back in the I Spy days.

On the other hand, it's just not acceptable for a black man to jump to a racist white man's defense. Even if it's one of your white relatives or someone you work for who's paid you a lot of money over the years. Hopefully, they understand why it's necessary for you to sever ties with them.

As the brand new commissioner, it was important for Adam Silver to act quickly and decisively. He didn't want to waffle on the issue and then just end up kicking the guy out of the league at a later date, like when Chuck D kicked Professor Griff out of Public Enemy, which maybe we'll discuss later in this book. Not only would that make him look weak, people might accuse him of being a racist, which again, would be an awkward thing for the white Jewish head of a league full of mostly black guys. Furthermore, tossing Donald Sterling under a bus helped nip this situation in the bud, before it turned into a referendum on the very idea of a league where most of the players are black and there's only one black majority owner.

With the racial disparity between team owners and players, and with the advent of Black People Twitter, it was inevitable that the Donald Sterling incident would lead to comparisons between the NBA and slavery. In fact, in some ways the NBA is similar to slavery, with the main difference being that NBA players are paid millions of dollars while slaves weren't paid a damn thing. Still, many NBA players just end up broke, the same way black people ended up broke once slavery ended. The government never did give us our 40 acres and a mule.

One thing I will say about slavery is that it was the one time in history when black unemployment approached zero. Not everyone can play in the NBA—I couldn't dunk a basketball, even in my prime, and my arms are almost long enough to touch the rim without jumping—but anyone can be a slave. Even if you were a fancy-pants classical music composer who somehow managed to avoid slavery, you could still end up getting kidnapped and shipped off to a plantation, like in Twelve Years a Slave.

As was the case in slavery, the level of control over NBA players' lives goes above and beyond what you'd experience in any other industry. Not only does the NBA control what players are allowed to wear during a game, they've got rules on what you're allowed to wear to and from the stadium and probably during the off season as well. I used to work in fast food back when you had to show up to your job on a Friday afternoon to get your check—that is, if you wanted to get high that weekend—before they started putting your check on a Rush Card-style debit card that probably charges you money out the ass to get your money in cash, and I was constantly surprised at the things people would wear. Guys would routinely show up in outfits that cost more than the amount of a two-week paycheck, which suggested to me that either they were supplementing their income by selling crack or their moms weren't charging them rent to live in the basement, or possibly both, and the girls would basically just show up naked. They'd show up with all kinds of shit hanging out of their clothes; things you wouldn't even see in a circa '02 rap video. The less business they had walking around half-naked, the more likely they were to walk around half-naked, and vice versa, because in areas that produce a lot of fast food employees, the larger a girl is, the more attractive she's considered, at least up to a certain point.

The NBA had to put the kibosh on guys walking around dressed like they were headed to sell crack after the game back during the Allen Iverson era. He'd had his share of problems before he even got in the league, and then once he did get in the league he had the sheer balls to try to release a rap album with lots of profanity, threats of violence and use of the other f-word, sometimes all in the same verse. It was actually kinda impressive, at least in that sense. Arguably, his song "40 Bars," with the lines, "Looking at me like them faggots be, I'll put you in the ground where maggots be," was the best song by an athlete other than "Must Be the Money" by Deion Sanders, the best song by an athlete of all time, of ALL TIME. True, Shaq had songs with many of the best rappers from the mid '90s, the best time ever for rap music, including the RZA and Biggie Smalls, but it's not like Shaq himself brought anything to those songs. Given a sufficient recording budget, I could have produced songs that were just as good.

There was also a problem with guys getting pulled over with weed in the car. Players would travel in caravans of three or four—maybe as many as seven or eight—luxury cars, and of course they'd end up getting pulled over by the police. One black guy in a luxury car is enough to be suspicious, let alone enough guys to play five on five with a few guys coming off the bench. Inevitably, they'd get pulled over, and sometimes the car with the NBA player in it would have weed in it. NBA players are sorta kinda allowed to smoke weed. It's not encouraged, but it's not tested for—as if this were UPS—either. In fact, some players find that it gives them a better sense of where the ball is headed on the court. They smoke up before games.

Back when I was in college, one team in particular, the Portland Trailblazers, seemed to have more problems with players getting busted for weed than any other team. This must have been because everyone smokes weed in Portland, where people in their 20s go to retire, and where the dream of the '90s is still alive, and also because there aren't very many black people in Portland who don't play for the Trailblazers. Who else are the cops going to pull over? It got to the point where the NBA was starting to look like a traveling gang of drug addicts, like Parliament-Funkadelic circa Mothership Connection, complete with cars that kinda looked like a spaceship made of cardboard and foil paper.

And so a meeting was held, in which then NBA commissioner David Stern announced a solution: From now on, if players are traveling in a caravan with umpteen other people, which of course they are, because black celebrities, the weed has to travel in a car separate from the NBA player. That way, if the car with the player in it got pulled over, he wouldn't have anything to worry about. If the car with the weed in it got pulled over, it would be nothing for a member of the player's entourage to take the rap, since his job just involves hanging out with a professional athlete. He doesn't have to sweat a possession offense or two on his record, and if he doesn't take the rap he'll be out of a job anyway. They could just have one guy in the car with the NBA player take the rap, but that only works if the guy who claims possession of the weed is black and everyone else in the car is white. If they're all black, they're all going to jail, regardless of whose weed it is. Ask T.I.

That really was an actual meeting. I remember hearing about it on TV. Later, in a frat house in Cape Girardeu, MO, birthplace of Rush Limbaugh and also where the movie Gone Girl is set—there's a big Rush billboard as you enter town, and I drank in the bar Ben Affleck owned in that movie—the term weed carrier was invented to describe a member of an NBA player's entourage whose job it is to claim possession of any marijuana if/when they're stopped by the police.

I didn't go to school down there, but my little brother and a few guys I went to high school with did, and I'd go down there to get wasted at the end of the semester or after the situation had deteriorated to a certain degree in Chicken Switch, MO, where my own school was located. Inevitably, the conversation would turn to some asinine argument about sports, and things I picked up during those arguments were the source of things I'd write about on my blog in the next few years, including the term weed carrier, which I adapted to describe members of a rapper's entourage who can't rap and yet were allowed to release albums back in the 'oos, before the bottom fell out of the industry, and the idea of the mindset of a champion as a sort of x factor that sets an athlete apart from another athlete with a more or less the same level of ability.

The NBA is also similar to slavery in that it places limits on players' political beliefs, or the beliefs they're allowed to express in public anyway. In actual slavery, of course slaves weren't allowed to believe that black people shouldn't be forced to work as slaves. Not that they were allowed to vote in elections or otherwise act on their beliefs. They couldn't do much other than pick cotton and sing old negro spirituals, and so they'd sing songs that sounded like the religious songs massa taught them to keep their behavior in check, but in fact contained covert messages about slitting massa's throat and making a run for it. They were the antebellum equivalent of rap music before it was co-opted, in that sense.

I can't imagine there would be an issue with, say, an NBA player endorsing a candidate in a presidential election who's already been thoroughly vetted by the Bilderberg Group and therefore allowed to run. I'm sure Obama's campaigns in 'o8 and '12 were less than ideal for a league that always has to be attentive to the needs of the kind of white people who are bothered by the idea of a grown black man who's allowed to pick out his own outfits, but as was the case with the vote to get rid of Sterling, they couldn't be seen telling black people they weren't allowed to endorse the first black presidential candidate who—as Joe Biden put it—was clean and articulate and therefore electable. It just wouldn't have looked right.

Where the NBA does draw the line is open expressions of support for, or solidarity with, Palestinians. In the summer of 2K14, when Israel launched its latest in a series of assaults on Gaza, Dwight Howard posted "#FreePalestine" on Twitter. In a matter of minutes, the tweet was gone and Howard was copping a plea. Either someone from the NBA had one of their contacts at Twitter go in and get rid of the tweet before Howard's five million followers started wondering what's Palestine, why wasn't it free in the first place, and why are we cutting checks to the tune of billions of dollars to keep it not free, when there's starving children here in the US, or they got on the phone with Howard and told him to delete it himself, lest he end up like that guy in the '90s who didn't want to stand up during the national anthem. If the NBA can easily get rid of the owner of a billion-dollar franchise, it's nothing for them to get rid of a player. As Don King would say, this is big business.

06.
Welcome To
The Terrordome

"Free Palestine."

— Rihanna

Rihanna must have seen what happened when Dwight Howard tried to tweet about the latest Israeli assault on Gaza and decided she'd tweet about it as well, to see what would happen.

Well, what happened was, as you may have guessed, that tweet lasted for all of about eight minutes, barely long enough for TMZ to screencap it for posterity and later run a series of blog posts on it. Either one of her handlers forced her to delete it, or they somehow got access to her account and deleted it themselves.

I wouldn't dismiss the latter as a possibility. Twitter can obviously go in and do whatever it wants with its own system, and for years now they've been attempting to cultivate a "special relationship" with the major labels, as part of their attempt to get anyone other than bored hoodrats and the tech community to use the site on a regular basis.

When Lyor Cohen's new 300 Entertainment was announced, it was mentioned that the label would have exclusive access to certain data from Twitter, presumably for the purpose of marketing its artists, but who knows what all they have access to and what they can use it for.

It's a known fact that Twitter saves a copy of everything you ever tweet, even if you go back and delete it, in case anyone from the government or an ad agency needs to take a look.

It's also well established that Rihanna is an habitual line stepper. She looks for opportunities to say and do things she doesn't have any business saying and doing... and that may or may not have led to the Rumble in the Lambo. Though obviously nothing she said or did could have justified what Chris Brown did to her face, and to be clear, I don't mean to suggest that it did.

Which is not to say that I don't have an idea of how the brother may have felt. The key is to extricate yourself from the situation. If she's egging you on, seemingly begging you to punch her in the face, simply walk away. Abandon your kids, if necessary. Women can raise kids by themselves, if they're not crazy, and if they are, there probably isn't much you can do anyway.

Of course the Rumble in the Lambo was complicated by the fact that it took place in a car—hence the name. He could have just gotten out of his car and walked away, like in REM's video for "Everybody Hurts" (how appropriate lol), which probably came out before his time, but that's an expensive car. You don't want to run the risk of someone stealing it, or her giving the keys to a homeless guy out of spite. The homeless know how to get rid of scrap metal. Both your car and the keys would be gone.

Lately, social media has been Rihanna's preferred outlet for provocation. She's known to go on Instagram and post topless pictures of herself that eventually have to be removed, in addition to numerous pics and videos of herself smoking weed and sniffing cocaine. At one point, her account had to be removed altogether.

I suppose whoring yourself out on Instagram beats antagonizing Chris Brown, if only because she's less likely to be assaulted as a result. She's too old to be duped into "human trafficking" and not have it be at least somewhat her fault, if not a conscious decision.

Rihanna's bold statement of solidarity with Palestinians just so happened to coincide with Trick Daddy declaring himself the CEO of the Eat a Booty Gang—an equally bold statement, I'd argue.

You get a lot of southern rappers saying weird sexual shit on social media, whether it's Kevin Gates talking about how he refuses to quit having sex with his cousin, Trick Daddy talking about how you shouldn't be afraid to eat a girl's ass, or Plies discussing his stretch-marks fetish. And there's probably even more than that. Those are just the ones I stumbled upon on Vlad TV, where I get a lot of my news.

I don't know what Trick Daddy's current label situation is. You hear all kinds of rumors about Trick Daddy dating back to the 1990s—that he's got any number of diseases, that he's dead, that he killed Trina for giving him AIDS. Trick Daddy rumors are the black equivalent of Richard Gere gerbil-in-the-ass rumors, and he's not on the Internets as often as he should be, despite having an album called www.thug.com, which only helps exacerbate the situation.

At any rate, there seemed to be minimal concern about a grown-ass man declaring himself the chief executive of an organization for people who eat ass. Trick Daddy's Eat a Booty Gang tweets remained online eight minutes after they appeared. There were no apologies issued or internal conspiracies to have them removed.

In fact, analingus was "having a moment," if you will, in the late summer of 2K14, both in hip-hop and in American popular culture in general, to the extent that the two don't completely overlap at this point. Trend pieces ran in New York magazine, GQ and Cosmo, along with a subsequent round of articles about whether or not you can ingest some sort of gross bacteria and probably die from sticking your tongue in someone's ass. Supposedly, it's more or less safe, if the girl—or guy, if that's your sort of thing—is clean.

Some stripper Drake banged claims he likes to have his salad tossed. Having your salad tossed, as explained in one of those great early to mid '90s-era HBO prison specials and later immortalized in Chris Rock's Bring the Pain, means having your ass eaten out with either jelly or syrup. The guy in the HBO prison special preferred syrup.

The stripper who claims that Drake likes to have his salad tossed didn't mention using jelly or syrup. Technically, he may not have had his salad tossed. I'll have to refer to the judges on that one, as well as a Pause Deputy. She did say that he's an expert on going down on a chick, more so than anyone else she'd been with—and presumably she'd been around the block a few times.

I'm not sure how appropriate that is for a famous rapper, let alone someone of Drake's status. To paraphrase the Tipper Gore surrogate in the movie Love Story, having a shedload of money means not being obligated to go down on a girl to get her to let you hit it. You can just hit it and pay her to leave, Charlie Sheen style.

The stripper says that once Drake got done doing his thing with her box, he rolled over and announced that it was his turn. She started giving him a blowski, but he kept forcing her head downward, first to his ballsack and then eventually to his ass, at which point his legs began shaking and he blew his load in her brand new weave.

I swear to god I didn't just make that up. It's from Media Take Out. (They made it up. lol) I would never just sit around and think of some shit like that, let alone subject you to it. I had to write that for the sake of journalism.

Tossing a salad, or rather eating someone's ass, not necessarily with jelly or syrup, later appeared in the otherwise kinda disappointing season four premiere of Girls, in early 2K15. The suspect folk singer guy Allison Williams' character was dating and also collaborating with bent her over a sink and went to town on her ass. It was promptly turned into an animated GIF that was all over the Internets the next day. I spent an entire afternoon staring at it.

Lena Dunham may have gotten the idea for that scene from a post on Gawker about eating ass. She has to check Gawker on the reg because they're constantly trolling her about her gross body, the latent racism on display in her work, the fact that she wouldn't have a career if it weren't for nepotism, so on and so forth.

She probably wasn't familiar with either the HBO prison special or Chris Rock's Bring the Pain, because she's half a decade younger than I am, and it seems like there's a lot of things she doesn't know about pop culture, for someone who makes TV shows for a living.

I just so happened to be on Twitter when she launched into a tirade about Woody Allen and his various children, stepchildren, wives, alleged abuse victims, and in some cases all of the above. Mia Farrow's daughter, Dylan or Satchel or whatever, the one he supposedly diddled, published an op-ed in the New York Times with no new details or convincing evidence, as part of a coordinated attempt both to sabotage the Oscar campaign for Blue Jasmine and promote Ronan Farrow's show on MSNBC.

It was obvious, from the way her Tweets were phrased, that Lena Dunham was just now learning that there had even been allegations against Woody Allen, and yet she seemed so certain that he was guilty, that he should be buried underneath the jail and his movies should be run over with the same steamroller they used to destroy gangster rap albums back in the early '90s.

Later that year, Bill Cosby's entire oeuvre really was destroyed "for all intensive purposes," removed from both TV Land and Netflix. It wasn't as tragic as it would be if you couldn't watch Woody Allen movies anymore, because the network TV sitcom is a garbage form of entertainment, and we're only about 10 years out from the point where young people won't even believe that people used to watch them, the power of Sofia Vergara's rack notwithstanding.

(Consulting the Google just now re: Ariel Winter, I see that she has her own subreddit. Of course she does.)

Ironically, Dunham was later involved in her own child abuse scandal. In her book Not That Kind of Girl she wrote about, among other things, taking a look inside her toddler sister's nether regions, apparently unaware that people might find that to be, at best, more information than they require, if not cause for the state to launch an investigation. If Woody Allen wrote the exact same thing, they really would bury him underneath the jail... and that's one of the many reasons to support #gamergate. Roffle.

One of the very few times I can recall a rap album being pulled from shelves for content was Mos Def's The New Danger. The one other example I can think of is of course Ice T's Cop Killer, which wasn't actually a rap album, but Ice T—at least back then—was mostly known as a rapper, and it's an important album in the history of rap music censorship, though the story behind it, since it doesn't involve anything sexual, is beyond the purview of this discussion.

The New Danger had that song "The Rape Over" on it, a parody version of Jay Z's classic Nas dis "The Takeover." On "The Rape Over," Mos complained about the state of rap music circa '04, which admittedly, is a popular topic for a certain kind of rapper in any given year. That year in particular, problems included corporate control over the content, rampant materialism and widespread drug use.

The part about rappers poking out their asses for a chance to cash in called to mind Bill Hicks' bits about artists of the late '80s and early '90s getting fucked in the ass by Satan, in what may have been a matter of great minds thinking alike.

The term tall Israeli was widely understood to refer to then Def Jam exec

Lyor Cohen. Cohen stands 6'5, which must make him amongst the tallest Jews to ever walk the earth, right up there with Aesop Rock. He's not Israeli, having been born here in the US, but he speaks with an Israeli accent, having lived in Israel for a period of time as a child after being abandoned by his parents.

Arguably, anyone who can pass for Jewish can be considered an Israeli, in that Israel will grant you citizenship and probably give you a free house in a settlement in the West Bank, while Palestinians who were kicked out in what's known as the Nakba aren't allowed to return to houses they still have the deed to.

Anyway, the rumor back then was that Lyor Cohen ordered all copies of The New Danger pulled from shelves and replaced with a version of the album without "The Rape Over" on it. The New Danger wasn't on Def Jam, but it wasn't inconceivable that an exec from another label could censor an artist. When Lyor forced Chuck D to kick Professor Griff out of Public Enemy, back in 1989, it was after he'd fielded calls from Jewish execs at other labels.

The New Danger was released on Rawkus Records, which by then was a subsidiary of Geffen Records, which was owned by Universal Music, the same company that owned Def Jam. The stories of artists having their careers put on hold on behalf of artists on other labels under the Universal Music umbrella are legion. Ask Ja Rule.

I attempted to Google Lyor Cohen having The New Danger pulled from shelves a while back, for another project I was working on, and all I could find was an article quoting someone from Rawkus/Geffen saying that the reason the album appeared to have been pulled from shelves and replaced was because there was a sample clearance issue that couldn't be settled before the album was released and therefore only the first few copies of the album sent to stores would have that song on it.

I could hardly find an example of a report that Lyor Cohen was the one who had the album pulled from shelves other than the one that ran on my own blog, which will be preserved for posterity for at least as long as I continue to pay the hosting fees. So maybe not that much longer, given the state of blogging as a business (if you will). You'll just have to take my word on the fact that this was fairly widely reported, at least by '04 hip-hop Internets standards.

After whatever happened with The New Danger, I began to use the term tall Israeli (or TI for short) to refer to white rap label execs, and more generally, to a secret cabal of individuals who control all facets of society, possibly operating from a bunker located six miles beneath the earth's surface.

Note that when I popularized the use of the term tall Israeli I wasn't aware that the Department of Homeland Security does in fact operate out of buildings in Washington, DC, that extend deep within the earth's surface, in part to hide the ridonkulous size of the agency.

2 Live Crew's As Nasty As They Wanna Be was never pulled from shelves, but some stores did refuse to sell it, while some stores actually got in trouble with the law for selling it. Ironically, a few people were arrested for selling the album in 2 Live Crew's native Florida, where drunk, half-naked college kids gather each spring to make sweet, passionate love in public.

Increasingly, this is captured on video and then circulated via Black People Twitter, and it's become an issue because it's not always clear that the girl is awake. EDM is often playing in the background, and it might be necessary to ban EDM, if that would prevent this from happening. I'd say it's worth a shot anyway.

2 Live Crew themselves were arrested for performing songs from As Nasty As They Wanna Be in a club. They were acquitted after Harvard professor Henry Louis "Skip" Gates, Jr., who later became famous for getting arrested for trying to break into his own house, thus prompting a Beer Summit between himself, the racist cop and Barack Obama, testified on their behalf in court, placing songs like "Me So Horny" and "The Fuck Shop" within the context of black literature.

It used to be that black intellectuals would defend rappers' freedom of speech on the grounds that rap music has a certain artistic value, and anyone trying to censor rap music is probably just a racist who doesn't want to see black people make money. And also, what kind of intellectual goes around advocating for censorship? Now black intellectuals are the main people trying to censor rap music, on the grounds that it's disrespectful to black women.

For what it's worth, rap music doesn't have as much artistic value as it used to.

In 1989, Professor Griff gave an interview to Moonie newspaper the Washington Times in which he accused the Jews of being responsible for most of the wickedness in the world. He must not have had his publicist there in the room with him.

Later he'd claim that he didn't realize that part of the interview was on the record, which I took to mean that he figured that the guy who conducted the interview, David Mills, a light-skinted black guy, wouldn't publish anything that could potentially cause him to get kicked out of the group. Sometimes black people get together and accuse the Jews of various crimes, and it's taken for granted this won't be repeated in mixed company.

Jesse Jackson ran into a similar problem in 1984, when he referred to New York as Hymietown while running for president. He was your one and only until he heard the news. Now he's sad and lonely since he put down the Jews.

I used to sorta kinda know David Mills, who's dead now. He used to read my blog back when he was a writer on The Wire. He somehow ascertained that I lived near where a meeting of white supremacists was being held and he tried to get me to conduct a reconnaissance mission. Because he could pass for white, he would actually show up to Klan rallies and shit. That was his hobby.

He may have been assassinated by the Illuminati. He dropped dead on the set of Treme (which apparently never recovered). He lived in DC, near where the ultra-secretive Bilderberg Group holds many of his meetings. The Illuminati has some sort of gun that causes you to have a heart attack and it looks like you just died of "natural causes" in your 40s, like Andrew Breitbart.

You would think that if the Minister of Information in your rap group (which has a Minister of Information) accused the Jews of being responsible of most of the wickedness in the world you could just issue an apology… and you'd be mistaken. Never ever issue an apology for anything; it's just a trap to get you fired from your job.

Rick Ross had to find out the hard way. He let feminists dupe him into issuing an apology for that song in which it sorta kinda seems like he's rapping about pulling a Bill Cosby on a girl. His apology was dismissed as not being good enough (pshaw!), and they ended up having to pretend like he'd been fired from his job as a spokesman for Reebok.

He was back in Reebok ads a few months later, but the point remains.

When Chuck D's apology for Professor Griff's comments (sometimes black people are forced to apologize for other black people's comments) was similarly dismissed, he then resorted to pretending as if Griff had been kicked out of the group. It was announced that Griff was no longer a member of Public Enemy, and then he was quietly allowed to rejoin a few weeks later.

Chuck D should have known that wouldn't work. When it didn't, he pulled a move later popularized by J Mascis from Dinosaur Jr. Rather than kick one guy out of the group, he disbanded the group altogether and then immediately reformed it with everyone who'd been in the group before except for one guy—in this case, Professor Griff.

At that point, in a stunning series of coincidences that I totally didn't just pull out of my ass, Professor Griff signed with Uncle Luke f/k/a Luke Skyywalker, lead vocalist of 2 Live Crew, released a few solo albums that literally no one bought and later became one of the hip-hop community's foremost experts on the Illuminati. If you've got an afternoon—or a lifetime, for that matter—in which you don't have shit else to do, check out a few of his videos on YouTube, including the one where he outs Will Smith as a down-low homosexual.

Every now and again Israel likes to rain down bombs and various illegal chemical weapons on the Gaza Strip, to thin out the herd and to reduce morale amongst the surviving populace.

They used to occupy Gaza militarily, but they had to give that up back in the mid '00s, because it got to be too much of a shit show. It's nice beachfront property, right there on the eastern end of the Mediterranean, but there must have been too many angry Palestinians and not enough space to establish illegal settlements.

I've heard Gaza described as being a little bit smaller than Seattle but with more than twice the population, which means they must be packed like sardines in a tin can. As the Gravediggaz might put it, there's nowhere to run to when Israel starts blowing shit up, which is why it's some ol' BS when the media—run by the TIs, natch—says that Hamas is using civilians as human shields. Western aid workers and the media are given advance warning to get TF out of dodge because there is no safe place to hide. The whole purpose of the attack is to kill civilians.

Operation Protective Edge began when three Israeli teenagers, attempting to hitchhike in the occupied West Bank, were kidnapped and eventually killed by members of Hamas. The stated justification for Operation Cast Lead, in late 2008 and early 2009, were "rocket attacks" that mostly just annoyed people and damaged the concrete facades of buildings, but in reality it was part of a deal with then president-elect Barack Obama, who agreed to look the other way, with the fact that he wasn't officially president yet serving as a convenient excuse.

George W. Bush fell off the wagon once the '08 presidential election got going full steam, perhaps under the impression that that meant his job here was done, and was hardly heard from the last few months he was in office. He was rumored to have been hitting the bottle the night he got that black eye and claimed he almost choked to death on a pretzel, but I've long suspected that he was a victim of reverse domestic violence. A few weeks after the '08 election, he was pictured down in Peru sipping a drink known as a Pisco Sour.

I watch Democracy Now! once or twice a week, if it looks like they've got something interesting on, as part of funemployment and also because I blame America first for anything bad that happens. I just so happened to be watching the day Operation Cast Lead kicked off, and I was taken aback by what I saw, particularly the stuff about the media and aid workers being allowed to leave before they started in with the carnage, and something about kids going blind either as a result of bombs going off or one of the chemical weapons they used. Note that this was a couple of years before I lost one of my own eyes.

Later that day, I was looking for something to write about for the blog I used to write for XXL and I saw a video of where Hot 97 DJ Peter Rosenberg had hosted a roundtable discussion about the Busta Rhymes song "Arab Money." Produced by Ron Browz, the guy who did "Ether," i.e. Nas' response to Jay Z's "The Takeover," "Arab Money" was controversial for a number of reasons, including its use of the term A-rab, which is frowned upon, its perpetuation of stereotypes about obscenely wealthy Arab guys, who fly Instagram thots around the world just to pee on them, and its chorus, which features Browz singing random Arab-sounding gibberish in Autotune.

In addition to Rosenberg himself, the roundtable discussion included this guy Mazzi, a blog rap-era industry gadfly perhaps most famous for writing a song about how the keffiyeh, as popularized by Rachael Ray, is not a "terrorist head scarf," who's Persian; a random Palestinian guy who may have been brought in off the street; and a Dominican guy who used to bring Cipha Sounds scarves and water, for when his brow was sweaty and his throat was parched.

At the very beginning of the video, Rosenberg jokes that he and the Palestinian guy just settled the Israeli-Palestinian conflict out in the hallway. In the blog post I wrote on it, I mentioned in passing that it was interesting to me that he would joke about such a thing, quite literally as the bombs were falling on Gaza, given that his father is a member of the Israel Lobby.

I was basing this on a picture I saw on his blog of his father having a conversation with Barack Obama. It looked like they may have been on stage somewhere at a campaign event. There was a fern or something in the background. I figured there was no way Obama would allow himself to be photographed with someone involved with Israel unless their views were thoroughly backwards. Earlier that year, there'd been an incident in which he was almost photographed in front of a mosque out in LA and had to take off running in the opposite direction.

According to Rosenberg, who saw my post and probably called someone at XXL and had it removed (though he denies this), I had his old man all wrong. His father wasn't a member of the Israel Lobby, he said, and in fact he had very progressive views on the Israeli-Palestinian conflict. Hmm...

Even though it didn't make sense to me why Obama would allow himself to be photographed sitting next to someone who has progressive views on the Israeli-Palestinian conflict, I was temporarily embarrassed. I have a tendency to fly off half-cocked with blog posts, which I'd argue, is what you're supposed to do with a blog post, rather than, say, with a book. More often than not, I'm right about these things, but sometimes I'm way wrong, and I figured that was the case here. After all, Peter Rosenberg wouldn't just lie and claim that his father wasn't a member of the Israel Lobby when I could very easily consult the Google and verify that he is, right? WRONG!

I briefly considered writing a post for my own blog in which I admitted that I was wrong about Rosenberg's old man. At that point, I hardly knew from Peter Rosenberg, and believe it or not, it's not my intent to purposely shit on people for no apparent reason. So I consulted the Google to see who Rosenberg's father actually was. According to a bio I found, he worked for a group called

Israel Policy Forum. That sounded to me like the name of one of the groups that make up the Israel Lobby, even though Peter Rosenberg said his father wasn't a member of the Israel Lobby, so I cross referenced it with a list of the groups that make up the Israel Lobby, per the book by Mearsheimer and Walt, via the entry for the Israel Lobby in the wiki, and come to find out it was one of those groups, with the caveat that this group in particular wasn't an according to Hoyle lobbying group in that it doesn't cut checks to politicians.

Which raises the question: How does a lobbying group influence policy if they don't cut checks? They must have a special version of the Zapruder film that's never been shown to the general public.

On my blog, and probably as an aside in umpteen other posts on my own blog and at XXL over the course of the next few weeks, I broke down how not only was Peter Rosenberg's father a member of the Israel Lobby, as I suspected when I saw that picture of him and Barack Obama, but Rosenberg the younger tried to lie and say he wasn't, and my dumb ass almost fell for it!

At that point, there was no way that Rosenberg could respond. There's no way you can argue with basic facts as listed in the world's most accurate encyclopedia. Instead he resorted to trolling me on Twitter and in interviews about my... shall we say, less than enviable personal life. In a video interview he did with some kid in what may have been Canada, he called me a fat loser who would never meet any famous rappers, which is the thing that I want most out of life, and who lives in a shanty town.

When I heard the part about the shanty town, I thought he might be referring to Combat Jack, with whom he'd also been beefing, because Combat Jack is Haitian, and this was during the Haiti earthquake in early '09, but Rosenberg assured me, via Twitter, that he was talking about me.

A few months later, I bought a house that cost about the same as a gently-used Buick and is about as nice a place to live. I've referred to it ever since, not quite affectionately, as my house in a shanty town.

07.
Picture Me Trolling

"Who am I gonna dis, if not black people?"

— Peter Rosenberg

A guy named Slowbucks somehow got on stage during G-Unit's set at Hot 97's annual Summer Jam and ended up getting beaten and robbed for his chain by some of 50 Cent's weed carriers. The whole thing was caught on tape and later went viral on the Internets.

If it wasn't the only part of Summer Jam 2K14 that was filmed, which seems less than likely in this day and age, it was the only thing anyone saw, and it may have been the most interesting thing that's happened at Summer Jam since Jay Z put a picture of Prodigy from Mobb Deep dressed as a ballerina up on the Jumbotron.

It's not uncommon for people who don't have any business being at Summer Jam in the first place, let alone on stage, to somehow slip through security. This might be a matter of Hot 97's security not being able to differentiate between black people. The year before, Papoose somehow got backstage and ended up performing as the headliner. He went on right as Kendrick Lamar's set was ending and played a few songs. Kendrick Lamar's set was naturally truncated, because the next good song he writes will also be the first good song he ever wrote. Hot 97 brass debated pulling the plug on Papoose, but they figured they might as well let him finish. It was the end of the evening anyway, so it was no big deal if people left. And if they'd interrupted his performance, one of his weed carriers might have popped a cap in someone's ass. If they couldn't keep Papoose from performing as headliner, there was no way of knowing if anyone there had a gun.

Slowbucks are a couple of guys from 50 Cent's hood who have a clothing line no one ever heard of. One of them's name is Winslow, or Slow, and the other one's name is Bugsy, or Bucks. Combine those two and you get Slowbucks, which is neither a word nor a desirable condition. I'm sure their clothes are similarly brilliant. Confusingly, Slow a/k/a Winslow is sometimes referred to as Slowbucks. He was the one who got his ass kicked at Summer Jam.

50 Cent once co-signed Slowbucks the clothing line in an obscure YouTube video, but they've since had a falling out due in part to the fact that Slowbucks the guy posed for a couple of pics on Instagram with Fiddy's archnemesis, Rawse, and also the fact that why should 50 Cent promote some guy's clothing line for free when he supposedly got $400 million to promote Vitamin Water? Rawse offered to co-sign Slowbucks, which supposedly helped them land a distribution deal, not because he believes in supporting young black entrepreneurs (where was he when I dropped Infinite Crab Meats?) but because he knew it would upset Fiddy.

50 Cent has been estranged from his son, Marquise, for a few years now. In 2012, he flew to Atlanta to spend some quality time with the boy, maybe take him fishing. When he pulled up to the house, he saw the lights go out and someone take off running, just like in the song "Found Out About You" by the Gin Blossoms. He banged on the door several times, but whoever was inside pretended like no one was home. Upset, he fired off a series of angry text messages. He said the kid's mother was the town bicycle back in the day, and therefore he wasn't even sure if he really was the father. He said he was getting a paternity test, and that he was through being a father either way. He signed off with, "Have a good life," or something to that effect.

Later, either Marquise or Shaniqua sold screencaps of the texts to some gossip blog. Fiddy copped a plea, saying he knew Shaniqua had taken the kid's phone. If so, it wouldn't be the first time a guy paid for his baby's mother's iPhone. I've worked in department stores on days when those child support checks would clear. I know how the game is played.

In the spring of 2K14, Marquise graduated from high school. 50 Cent didn't show up. Marquise wrote on Instagram that he was under the impression that Fiddy would be there, but he wasn't surprised that he wasn't. Contacted by paparazzi, Fiddy said he didn't know when the graduation was or where it would be held; otherwise, he would have been there. A few weeks later, pics emerged of Biggie Smalls' son, CJ, at his own high school graduation, holding some white kid from behind like they were bufuing, leading to rumors that he might be a fudge. Many rappers' sons either aren't sufficiently masculine or have decidedly unfortunate facial hair, including Ghostface's son Infinite Coles a/k/a Infinite Poles; DMX's son, who was on an episode of Iyanla Vanzant's show on Oprah Winfrey's deep cable network; and at least one of Snoop Dogg's sons.

Not long before Summer Jam, Marquise posed for an Instagram pic with Slowbucks. Fiddy himself appeared in the comments section, declaring that this was a bad idea, leading to speculation that Fiddy might have one of his weed carriers pop a cap in Slowbucks' ass or burn down his house.

In the weeks following the incident at Summer Jam, it was announced that Slowbucks was suing 50 Cent. He held a press conference in a room that looked just like the break room at a Kmart where I used to work. I googled the name of his lawyer, and come to find out, the guy mostly deals with patents. He must be one of Slowbucks the guy's distant relatives.

Chuck D must have seen the video of Slowbucks getting beaten and robbed live on stage. On Twitter, he called Summer Jam 2K15 "a sloppy fiasco." Chuck D has been touring with Public Enemy for like 30 years, and never has anyone been robbed on stage during his performance—and he's in a group with Flavor Flav!

Other problems Chuck D had with Summer Jam 2K14 included the line-up, which he didn't find to be old enough or New York enough, and the fact that artists were allowed to use the dreaded n-word. He said there was no way artists would be allowed to use anti-Semitic slurs... which may or may not be true. Someone would have to try it.

Imagine if Chuck D had actually attended Summer Jam 2K14. He would have been highly upset! It may have been necessary for him to have a word with someone in charge, and I'm not sure if they would have let him backstage. He's black and sometimes he wears a ball cap, but he's too old to be a performer. No one would believe he was someone's father, because black people.

The next day, Peter Rosenberg went off on Chuck D, in a segment on the

Hot 97 morning show called The Realness, calling him a troll and irrelevant and questioning his contribution to hip-hop. He said he does more for hip-hop than Chuck D, and he wondered why anyone should give a shit what Chuck D says.

The Internets didn't appreciate Rosenberg's disrespectful tone or the suggestion that he does anything at all worthwhile for hip-hop, let alone more than Chuck D, the guy who made It Takes a Nation of Millions to Hold Us Back.

Video of Rosenberg going off on Chuck D, uploaded to YouTube by Hot 97, became major news on the hip-hop Internets, in the way that a gay rumor or video of a group of hoodrats duking it out at McDonald's is major news on the hip-hop Internets—it was all over the place. Rosenberg was often presented as the white cultural interloper, who clearly has no respect for the black pioneer. These articles were highly accurate.

Ironically, if the purpose of Peter Rosenberg going off on Chuck D was to have people think that Summer Jam 2K14 wasn't a sloppy fiasco, it ended up having the opposite of its intended effect. Many people weren't even aware that Slowbucks had been robbed until the Rosenberg video went viral. I'm sure Slowbucks wishes it hadn't.

You'll recall that something similar happened with the term tall Israeli, which became hip-hop Internets shorthand for who really runs rap music, after Lyor Cohen allegedly had copies of Mos Def's The New Danger pulled from shelves.

On the Internets, this phenomenon is known as the Streisand effect, after an incident in which Barbara Streisand tried to have some pictures of her house removed from the Internets, so people wouldn't know where she lives, which only resulted in most people on the Internets at the time—the vast majority of whom could give a rat's ass where Barbara Streisand lives—finding out where she lives. Hopefully, she got robbed.

In the '70s, this never would have been an issue. There really were certain individuals in the media who could have information suppressed. That may have been who Barbara Streisand thought she was calling. She didn't understand how the Internets work. She's an old-ass lady.

If the way Rosenberg addressed Chuck D hadn't been so disrespectful, it's likely that some people would have agreed with him. Chuck D really does sit around on Twitter all day and bitch and moan about the current state of hip-hop. Personally, I find that he shares some valuable information, and the current state of hip-hop is one of my favorites topics to discuss. I hope to be doing the exact same thing when I'm in my 50s, if there's still such a thing as Twitter and I haven't already long since dropped dead from a massive coronary.

Lest we forget, Chuck D is the same guy who sued Biggie Smalls' corpse, and also DJ Premier, for sampling his voice on the song "10 Crack Commandments." As if Biggie's corpse didn't have enough problems; it sprung a leak en route to New York from LA, where his funeral was held, which I'm sure was decidedly unpleasant. What part of the rap game is that, suing another rapper for sampling your voice on a song? I don't care if the song is about how to sell crack. Chuck D has a crackhead in his group, and he brought him around to all 50 states and many foreign countries, putting the entire world's VCRs at risk.

Rosenberg was left with no choice but to cop a plea on Twitter. He tried to pull what's known as a Jedi mind trick, in which you say you didn't do some shit we just saw you do. In this case, anyone who saw him tweet that he would never compare his contribution to hip-hop to Chuck D could very easily pull up the video of him saying that he contributes more to hip-hop than Chuck D. You had to be on an Internets-connected device to even see the tweet, unless someone printed it out for you—which might be how Barbara Streisand uses Twitter.

Rosenberg may have been counting on hip-hop websites slavishly screen-capping his tweet and presenting it as news, with the headline, "Peter Rosenberg never said he did more for hip-hop than Chuck D," or something to that effect. That's how a lot of hip-hop journalism is made these days. The top websites have teams of kids over in India who screencap tweets related to trending topics. They present 30 or 50 of these tweets in a slideshow, and they make a few pennies every time you click on the next one. They could give a rat's ass about the veracity of the information presented. Legally, they can't be sued if it turns out to be some ol' bullshit, because it's considered user-generated content. This is based on a law passed back in like '96.

Clearly, Peter Rosenberg doesn't have a very high opinion of the hip-hop community's intellectual ability, if he thought he could just tell people he didn't do something everyone just saw him do, and ironically, that may have also contributed to the backlash against him.

In the late '00s, Muammar Gaddafi, longtime dictator of Libya, visited New York to deliver an address to the United Nations, possibly to put people on notice—to deliver his own version of The Realness, if you will.

Hotel owners in New York found out about this and didn't want to give him a place to stay. Some people still hold him responsible for an airplane that was blown up over Scotland, Pan Am Flight 103, as referenced on the song "Gold" by the GZA, on Liquid Swords, one of the best rap albums of all time. The GZA, who mentions Richard Nixon on the first Wu-Tang album, is known to take it back. He's the oldest member of the Clan. No one gave a shit that the GZA made light of a terrorist attack in which hundreds of people were killed, because that was back when only black people and cool white people listened to rap music. There was hardly such a thing as the Internets.

Muammar Gaddafi didn't blow up Pan Am Flight 103, but the US probably wanted him to extradite random Libyans who had been implicated, to hook jumper cables up to their balls, like in the thoroughly CIA-vetted propaganda film Zero Dark Thirty. There was a lot of racism and propaganda against Libyans in the 1980s. I'm pretty sure the Arab guys who killed Doc Brown in the first Back to the Future—because they hired him to make a bomb and he used the plutonium to make the flux capacitor, which is what makes time travel possible—were Libyans.

When Gaddafi couldn't find a place to stay, he threatened to pitch a tent in Central Park. I think he used to be in the military, so it would have been nothing for him to sleep outdoors. He was commonly referred to as Colonel Gaddafi, but you never can tell with these dictators. They like to cultivate an image of being capable warriors. Some of them dress as if they're about to lead an army into battle, despite never having been in the military a day in their lives. That's why I fuxwit Mahmoud Ahmadinejad: he wears a Member's Only jacket, known as the Ahmadinejacket, and he still somehow manages to instill fear in the heart of the West. It's probably been customized by the Iranian military to be bulletproof and immune to explosive cigars and what have you, not to mention treated with Scotchgard, in case he spills coffee on it. They can't have him out here with stains on his jacket, looking like he's slept in it since 1996.

Ultimately, I'm pretty sure Gaddafi did end up getting a hotel room somewhere. It was just a little bit off the beaten path. Something similar happened to Fidel Castro back in the '60s. He came to New York for diplomacy purposes or whatever, and the hotels wouldn't let him get a room. He ended up staying in Harlem, where he met with Malcolm X. If Malcolm X had lived, the two of them might have joined forces to try to finally get black people some rights in this damn country, and that's one of the reasons why the FBI and the NYPD, who had Malcolm X under surveillance for years, either had him killed or turned a blind eye when the honorable Elijah Muhammad had him killed. The last thing the government wants is black people here in the US acting in solidarity with people in other countries who are oppressed by the US and its satellite office in the Middle East, Israel.

Which brings us to Peter Rosenberg. When it was announced that Gaddafi might have to pitch a tent in a park, two years before Occupy Wall Street, Rosenberg went on the radio—on Hot 97, a station that plays rap songs about selling and doing drugs, shooting people and disrespecting women, along with garbage pop songs that don't have any business on a hip-hop station—and announced that Muammar Gaddafi shouldn't have been allowed to address the UN in the first place, because he's a terrorist and a killer of children.

Combat Jack's thing back then was to troll people on the radio. For a period of time, there was no proper Hot 97 morning show to speak of; they were running this guy Big Boy, who did the morning show on Power 106 in LA, which is owned by the same corporation as Hot 97, Emmis Communications out of Indianapolis, not to be confused with Power 105 in New York, Hot 97's crosstown rival. Combat says that Big Boy in the Morning, in addition to being kinda gay-sounding, was neither a very good show nor was it appropriate for New York.

Immediately prior to that had been a period of controversy and turmoil for Hot 97. They used to run a feature called Smackfest, where they'd bring hood-rats into the studio and have them smack the shit out of each other, and sometimes they'd start going at it and the cops would have to be called. There were multiple shootouts in the lobby and in the street outside the building where the station is located, involving Lil Kim, G-Unit and the guy who played Biggie Smalls in the Biggie Smalls biopic, who got shot in the ass trying to harass people into listening to his demo tape in the street outside the station and then went upstairs and spit a freestyle with a gunshot wound in his ass. It was later rumored that he had someone shoot him in the ass on purpose, as a publicity stunt. There was an episode of The Sopranos about that back in the dark ages of the early 2000s. I think Lord Jamar may have been in it. Before Lord Jamar was on The Sopranos, he was on OZ, where he had to film a scene in which he showered naked with other guys. People sometimes post screencaps of it on Twitter when Jamar declares that gay shit has no place in hip-hop.

And who can forget the Tsunami Song, the hilarious tribute to victims of a tsunami that hit Indonesia or somewhere back in the mid '00s, umpteen global warming-related natural disasters ago? The Tsunami Song included lyrics like "you can hear the screaming chinks" and "now your children will be sold into child slavery." Some people didn't see the humor in this, and it resulted in protests in the street outside the station, where people could have been shot, and sponsors pulling their ads. Ultimately, one of the show's producers, who wrote the song, and the late Todd Lynn, who used to read my blog, and who threatened to shoot Miss Info, who'd objected to the Tsunami Song, lost their jobs.

The building Hot 97 was in was owned by a construction workers pension fund. It may have just been a front for the mafia. The building was trying to have Hot 97 evicted, and Hot 97 alleged that these were just strong-arm tactics to try to jack up their rent; the fact that shootouts were taking place in the lobby was neither here nor there. At a certain point, they had to give Hot 97 its own separate elevator, lest someone taking an elevator to one of the other floors was robbed or sexually assaulted. White guests and employees of Hot 97 weren't prevented from taking the non-Hot 97 elevator to visit the studio, leading to allegations of racism.

It was decided that Hot 97 needed to whiten up its image. Black people had been driven out of New York for years, with the rise of housing prices and stop and frisk, and they couldn't risk any more problems with their landlord, whether it was shootouts in the lobby or the cops having to be called to break up hoodrat brawls in the studio. Enter Peter Rosenberg. Peter Rosenberg had been a college radio DJ at the University of Maryland. His career as a professional hip-hop radio host was a nonstarter. He hosted a talk program on a station in the town where he went to college. By the time Hot 97 found him, he'd been reduced to making parody videos on YouTube. Now he's a morning show host on what was once the top hip-hop station in the biggest market in the country. Nothing like that ever happens to black people.

Combat Jack was listening to Peter Rosenberg on the Hot 97 Morning Show, in the car with his kids, when Rosenberg announced that Gaddafi shouldn't have been allowed to address the UN in the first place. It didn't make sense to Combat why Rosenberg was on Hot 97 discussing whether or not Muammar Gaddafi should be allowed to address the UN, and he found Rosenberg's tone to be disrespectful, in much the same way that people found Rosenberg's comments about Chuck D disrespectful. It wasn't uncommon back then to go on Twitter and see Rosenberg saying a lot of off-brand shit about prominent black men, like Bobby Brown and Al Sharpton. He called Al Sharpton an ambulance chaser, during Michael Jackson's funeral. He would argue that Al Sharpton extorts money from companies accused of racism, or that Bobby Brown is alleged to have put a shoe on Whitney Houston, but you got the sense that he just lives to talk shit about black men, and that he merely cited whatever personal problems those guys may have had for plausible deniability purposes.

On Twitter, Combat told Rosenberg that Muammar Gaddafi deserves respect both as a head of state and as a human being. No human should be forced to pitch a tent in a park to have somewhere to stay, unless he wants to, I would add. To this, Rosenberg responded, out of the blue, that he would slap the shit out of Combat in front of his kids.

The idea that Rosenberg would slap the shit out of someone seemed ridiculous, because he's not a very big guy, despite seeming constantly bloated, like someone who doesn't realize that his body can't properly digest milk. I bet he farts in bed constantly, and his wife—a blonde deep-cable sports reporter—only puts up with it on the basis of the strength of those Hot 97 checks. Combat Jack is five years older than he says he is in interviews, but aside from the weird, exhausted facial expression Combat has in most photographs, they appear to be more or less the same age.

And I'm at a loss for what the kids had to do with it. Was the idea that it might be necessary, strategically, to have Combat's kids present, that otherwise the prospect of getting slapped by Peter Rosenberg might not be sufficient to get him to change his views on Muammar Gaddafi?

It wasn't the first time a New York hip-hop radio host brought someone's kids into it. Years before, Star, one of Rosenberg's predecessors, was arrested for threatening to pull an R. Kelly on DJ Envy's daughter, while he was hosting the morning show at Power 105. He also called Envy's wife, who's part-Asian, a slanty-eyed hoo-er.

Star had hosted the morning show at Hot 97 back in the early 2000s, and it's rumored that he was let go for showing up high and drunk and demanding exorbitant amounts of money. Star is Combat Jack's idol and also my own idol. I highly recommend his book Objective Hate. Star was then hired by Power 105, where he battled the Hot 97 morning show for ratings. In fact, that's why Hot 97 came up with the Tsunami Song. DJ Envy is now a host of Power 105's morning show The Breakfast Club. Back then he was with Hot 97.

Ironically, Star did more time for threatening to pull an R. Kelly on someone's kid than R. Kelly did for actually peeing on a middle school-age girl. Rosenberg wasn't investigated, let alone arrested, for threatening to slap the shit out of Combat Jack in front of his kids, though arguably that may have been more traumatic for them than getting peed on was for that girl. Young though she may have been, she seemed like she'd been peed on before and that she enjoyed it. As Arruh himself would say, it seemed like she was ready (to be peed on).

––––––

A few weeks later, Combat was hired to co-host Shade 45's morning show, on Sirius XM satellite radio, with Angela Yee, now one of the hosts of Power 105's ascendant Breakfast Club. Combat Jack is good at getting a high profile job in entertainment media and only holding on to it for a brief period of time. Over the years, he's been the managing editor of The Source, an exec with MTV, host of a TV show for Complex, so on and so forth, not to mention whatever corporate law jobs he took after he shut down his entertainment law practice supposedly because he was tired of being a lawyer. His stint with Shade 45 holds the all-time record for brevity, and as alluded to in my first book, The Mindset of a Champion, it's all my fault.

Combat told Angela Yee that he used to be a lawyer, which is what he tells everyone he meets, and that after that he wrote blog posts for some blog called ByronCrawford.com: The Mindset of a Champion. Angela Yee told this to

Eminem's manager Paul Rosenberg, not to be confused with Hot 97 morning
show host Peter Rosenberg, though I'm sure they're somehow related, and that
must have set off an alarm in his mind.

Over the years, I've had my share of disagreements with Elliott Wilson,
founder of RapRadar. He was my boss at XXL. When Elliott was let go from
XXL, supposedly because they found coke in his desk, he announced that he
was starting his own blog, RapRadar. It took like a year, or maybe longer than
that, for RapRadar to launch, and it didn't make sense to me why it would take
that long to start a blog. It's so easy to start a blog that Tumblr has a limit on the
number of blogs you're allowed to start in one day, and it's like 100.

I did a whois search on the domain for RapRadar, and come to find out, it's
owned by Goliath Artist Management, in New Jersey, one of Paul Rosenberg's
companies. It wasn't until a while after RapRadar launched that Elliott copped
to the fact that it's owned by Paul Rosenberg. They were trying to keep that
under wraps.

In the early days of RapRadar, they ran an angry editorial complaining that
Eminem wasn't included in MTV's annual list of the hottest MCs in the game.
This was back when Relapse was out, and people weren't really fuxxing with
Relapse, even though it's still the best thing he's done since he reemerged. No-
where in this article was it mentioned that RapRadar is owned by Eminem's
manager Paul Rosenberg.

A blog called ANIMAL somehow got its hands on an email in which Paul
Rosenberg ordered Elliott Wilson to post a new song by Eminem, thus proving that Paul Rosenberg doesn't just own RapRadar, he uses it as a personal
PR apparatus for Eminem, and probably whoever else he manages as well. I
posted screencaps of the email on my blog. An upset Elliott called ANIMAL
and demanded that his boss' email address be blurred out or removed, before
he was deluged with solicitations from bum rappers, in a conversation that was
recorded for posterity. I posted the audio on my blog. I'm thinking Rosenberg's
email address must have eventually been obscured or removed, because I still
get email from people wanting me to put them in contact with Paul Rosenberg,
and why would they need to ask if his address was still somewhere on my blog.

There may have also been concern with something I posted about how Paul
Rosenberg sorta kinda killed DJ AM. DJ AM played huge nightclubs in Las

Vegas and was known for his involvement in that mid to late 'oos-era celebu-
tante milieu. I think he dated either Paris Hilton or Nicole Richie. He might
also be credited for either inventing or popularizing the mashup, where a DJ
takes two songs from different genres and edits them together for irony purposes. Or maybe he just played mashups? I wouldn't know. I would never pay to
see someone DJ.

Paul Rosenberg was DJ AM's manager and also executive producer on a
show on MTV where they had AM handling crack rocks. I think the idea was
to have AM, a former crackhead, explain to kids the importance of not doing
drugs. Handling drugs on the show caused him to relapse, and he died of an
overdose shortly thereafter. It was argued that AM should have never been on
the MTV drug show in the first place, and that Rosenberg being both AM's
manager and executive producer on the show constituted a conflict of interest.
AM shouldn't have been around drugs, but Rosenberg would have lost money
by pulling him from the show.

It's also alleged that Rosenberg was aware that AM had relapsed, which
contradicts statements to the press that he had no idea AM was back on drugs.
AM had two managers, and when he died, the other manager was attempting
to stage an intervention. Rosenberg wanted to postpone it until they were done
taping the show. Keep in mind, this is all according to information someone
sent me via DM on Twitter. It may or may not be true. I don't know Paul
Rosenberg personally to be able to say if he seems like Rap Game Frank Un-
derwood, i.e. the kind of guy who would risk someone's life just to make a few
extra dollars from MTV, when he's already got all of that Eminem money.

At the time, I was under the impression that a lot of prominent hip-hop
journalists received the same information about Paul Rosenberg that I received, and I was just the only one to run with it. I never really sweated the
consequences of anything I posted because I never had a job that paid a living
wage a day in my life. Why not put the TIs on blast? If it's true that the post
on AM had anything to do with Combat being let go from Sirius before he
began, that would explain why everyone else was reticent to write about it. It
makes you wonder what else these so-called journalists know that they aren't
writing about.

08.
Bring On The Major Leagues

"It's no offense to transgender women, but I only get with transgender women for one thing and one thing only, and that's for oral sex."

— Mister Cee

I was still blogging for XXL back then, and for a period of time Combat began blogging there as well. He wrote a post, about how he doesn't really fuxwit 2Pac musically, that got a rise out of the Internets. That job lasted for about as long as it took for Combat to realize that we didn't always get paid.

Rap magazines were always notorious about not cutting checks. XXL was probably in a better position financially than the rest of them, but it was run by people who weren't the sharpest pencils in the box, and there was a lot of turnover. You were never quite sure whom you worked for or whom to contact if your check didn't show up, especially if, like me, you lived in Missouri and never once visited the XXL offices. I don't even think I had the phone number. Sometimes you wouldn't get a check for a month or two and then the next month you'd get a check for that month and also the months they skipped. I viewed every check I ever received from XXL as getting over on someone, so I couldn't be too upset. Combat Jack, on the other hand, is a wealthy former entertainment lawyer. He had little tolerance for people not paying him for his work. Apparently, his conversations with XXL brass were somewhat contentious in nature.

From there, it was on to an obscure blog owned by a guy from an indie-rap label that's famous for jerking its artists... supposedly. I was told that this site paid better than XXL, and I seriously considered ditching XXL to work there, both while Combat was there, circa '09, and after I was let go from XXL, in early 2K11. I talked to the guy on the phone once at like 5 AM. It was an awkward conversation that never really went anywhere, and that was the end of that. By that time, Combat was the managing editor of The Source, i.e. the guy who hired writers, but there was no way he was going to hire me, after what happened with Sirius. Paul Rosenberg had found a way to fuck me after all. No homo. The people Combat did end up hiring were clowns, and he was gone from that job, for whatever reason, in a year or so, not having done anything particularly worthwhile.

Combat Jack is one of the best writers I've ever read, hands down. He's a truly miserable announcer, so it's ironic he's become so gung ho about podcasting. His voice, diction, breath control and what have you are no good. I was hoping he'd get a chance to flex his skills as a writer in The Source, but the few things he did that I saw were just the same BS articles you always see in The Source. When he was let go, it must have come as a surprise to him. There seems to be bad blood between him and Londell McMillan, the guy who owns The Source. If only he'd known his days at The Source were numbered, maybe he could have gotten me in there as he was walking out the door, if only to fuck Londell. No Michael Sam.

In 2K10, Combat again set his sights on radio. First he attempted to patch things up with Peter Rosenberg. Rosenberg invited him up to Hot 97 to have a conversation about their beef, which they would record and upload to the Internets as a podcast. Combat may have been under the impression that this might lead to a job at Hot 97. I don't know that he's given up hope of working at Hot 97, to this day, despite subsequent issues he's had with various people there. He's an optimistic person.

This podcast, as I recall, consisted of Rosenberg explaining why he threatened to slap Combat Jack in front of his kids, which I'm sure he blamed on me, and Combat explaining, Dr. Phil-style, how he felt when Rosenberg threatened to slap him in front of his kids. Then they held hands and sang Kumbaya. If Combat wanted to take off his shoe and beat Rosenberg with it on GP, he wasn't about to, lest it ruin his career prospects. The power imbalance in that room was as palpable as it was gross, like going to your dad's job and watching his boss order him around. I think there was once an episode of The Wonder Years about that.

Later that year, Combat launched the Combat Jack Show, first as an Internets-radio show with PNC, an Internets-radio station, and later as the podcast we all know and love, available on Soundcloud and iTunes. It started out with just Combat and Dallas Penn in a room, shooting the shit and making fun of A-King, a guy from PNC. That was when it was at its best. It's had its moments in its current format, which is a knockoff version of Rosenberg's Juan Epstein podcast with Cipha Sounds, but it's also had some truly terrible moments, which were unnecessary for any reason other than to try to juice the stats, to make money from advertising. In between now and then, there was a morning zoo format inspired by the Howard Stern Show, complete with recurring bits, music breaks and a guy reading the news. That was when the show was at its absolute worst.

Brian "B.Dot" Miller is the kid who does a lot of the posts on RapRadar a/k/a RapPravda. Elliott Wilson is the site's nominal black-ish figurehead, but I'm not sure how involved he is with the day to day, which doesn't involve anything other than copying and pasting the embed code for YouTube videos into a little text window. Admittedly, that's all I do with my own site more often than not, though I'd argue that curating twerk videos and pictures of girls with a certain look requires more effort than you'd think. And of course Paul Rosenberg (and maybe also Eminem) owns the site, and works out the various scams in which ad budgets for companies he deals with like Interscope Records and Sirius XM's Shade 45 are funneled into the site's coffers.

In the early days of RapPravda, I remember B.Dot tried to write an actual article. It was all about how he doesn't find the late, great J Dilla to be a very good producer. It's one of the worst things you'll ever read about rap music. He's since become famous for not liking MF Doom either, though I'm not sure if this is the result of another article he wrote or something he said on Twitter. He's known for mixing it up on Twitter. He was a constant presence on my TL a while back, but it's been years since I've seen so much as a random stray tweet from him. He may have blocked me. I'd check, but I don't need to hear anything he has to say. If he's involved in some sort of beef, I'm sure I'll hear about it through the proverbial grapevine.

In 2012, he famously called a guy named Jordan Sargent a cultural tourist for giving a Chief Keef album an 8 out of 10 in a review for SPIN, after a Nas album received 7 out of 10 from SPIN earlier that year, leading to a discussion about whether or not white people should be allowed to write about rap music. I believe that people of all races should be allowed to write about rap music, because I'm not a racist, but I wonder: Why would anyone want to read something a white person wrote about rap music? This was a year or two before Lord Jamar famously declared that white people are guests in the house of hip-hop and therefore it's inappropriate for them to try to push a gay agenda. B.Dot was out ahead of this trend. Credit where credit is due. Jordan Sargent seems like he might be gay. Note that I don't mean that in the sense that I don't like him and therefore I'm suggesting that he's gay. I don't know the guy from a can of paint. But I've seen where he's written a few suspect articles for Gawker, about guys' cocks, rent-boy parties and what have you. Nullus. If he is straight, hopefully they don't have him in there sucking people's dicks to keep his job. It's a tough economy, and I heard gay guys do shit like that.

Later that year, B.Dot complained on Twitter that Hot 97 doesn't play enough local artists and underground artists. I'm not sure which underground artists he could have been referring to, at least in the boom-bap dinosaur sense of the term underground, if he doesn't like Dilla and MF Doom. He may have been referring to garbage, provincial New York rappers who remain obscure primarily due to a lack of talent, like Troy Ave a/k/a Troy Average, who could be considered both local and underground. Combat Jack championed Troy Ave a while back, in what must have just been a matter of mistaken trend-humping, and it ended up coming back to bite him in the ass, when Troy Ave shit on him on Power 105's The Breakfast Club. Troy Ave was upset that Combat didn't want to name him rookie of the year in some BS roundtable discussion, because he's been around in some form or another since back in the '00s.

On the radio the next day, then Hot 97 Program Director Ebro, in the same segment in which Peter Rosenberg would later shit on Chuck D, explained why Hot 97 has to play the same artists 15 times a day for three months and can't play local and underground artists. Using Sean Price as an example for some reason, he said that underground rappers, whom he called minor-league rappers, weren't ready to be played on Hot 97, at least during the day, because they'd yet to make a song that's palatable to girls, children and white people, all of whom need their hip-hop watered down some—which, to his credit, is true. Until then, they'd have to settle for Peter Rosenberg's underground show, Real Late, which airs between the hours of midnight and 2 AM on Monday mornings, a time when even people who don't do shit but sit around and get high are likely to be sleeping.

People on the Internets had already been bitching and moaning about Hot 97, and this segment only had the effect of pouring gasoline on the fire, so to speak. Ebro's explanation of why they can't just play Sean Price during the day as if this were 1996—when the song "Leflaur Leflah Eshkoshka" by Heltah Skeltah and OGC, as the Fab Five, one of the best songs of all time, was briefly popular—may have been true, but it was hardly satisfying. Why should people who sit around on Twitter all day give a rat's ass if Hot 97 makes more money playing Katy Perry songs? I'm sure they could make even more money running scams on the elderly. Does a radio station not have a certain obligation to the community it serves? Sean Price himself eventually caught wind of the segment and changed his name on Twitter to Minor League Rapper.

One of the things Combat likes to do is insert himself in the middle of two people who are beefing on the Internets, usually on social media sites like Twitter and Instagram, and then offer The Combat Jack Show as a venue to work out their differences. I already broke down, in Infinite Crab Meats, how this led to the legendarily awful first Rap Genius episode (not to be confused with the legendarily awful second Rap Genius episode), and if you're lucky, maybe I'll break down elsewhere in this book how this tactic led to the legendarily awful Return of Dame Dash episode, not be confused with the first Dame Dash episode, which was easily one of the top five episodes of The Combat Jack Show of all time, of ALL TIME.

When conversation on Twitter turned to Hot 97 being a garbage radio station and not playing enough quote-unquote real hip-hop, it was an excellent opportunity for Combat Jack to generate publicity for The Combat Jack Show and also to participate in an important conversation about the current state of hip-hop, which is the most important thing in the world at any given moment, if most interviews with rappers are any indication. In order to facilitate this, he created the hashtag #OccupyHot97, based on Occupy Wall Street, which took place around the same time a year before, so that his tweets about the station would be easily searchable and also to troll Ebro, Rosenberg, et al.

Eventually, Combat's tweets caught Ebro's attention, and either he felt the heat from #OccupyHot97 and decided it was necessary to go on The Combat Jack Show and defend himself or he figured it might be a good opportunity to generate publicity for himself the same way Combat was trying to generate publicity for the show. (Podcasts are all about generating publicity, especially for garbage rap albums.) Rosenberg may have let him know that there wasn't any real risk of Combat taking him to task. At any rate, Combat invited Ebro on the show to talk about minor league rappers, #OccupyHot97 and what have you, and Ebro accepted... with the caveat that Combat and the three or four guys who were taking up space in the studio with him at the time come down to Hot 97, rather than Ebro going to wherever they were recording The Combat Jack Show at the time. At various points, it's been recorded at Internets-radio station PNC, a recording studio owned by one-time co-host Just Blaze and Engine Room Audio, a recording studio in lower Manhattan that appears to just be a closet with a microphone and a few folding chairs in it. Hot 97 has all kinds of fancy equipment for putting together radio shows, and they've got restrictions on who's allowed in the studio, from when they were having "issues," back in the mid '00s. You never know who might be at, say, PNC. In the early days of The Combat Jack Show, there were times when random guys would just wander into the studio and become guests on the show.

This episode didn't really consist of much other than Ebro explaining to Combat Jack and crew how a large corporate hip-hop radio station worked circa 2012. Basically, they get playlists from a room full of white guys in Indiana, who have access to all kinds of data and marketing equipment, and they have to stick to those playlists, or else people would change the station, or more likely, Ebro would just get fired and replaced with someone who wouldn't veer from the corporate-mandated playlists. They have a little more leeway in the wee hours of Monday morning, when only nocturnal animals that have to root through the garbage for sustenance are awake, and that's why they put Rosenberg's underground rap show there. Really, they could play anything they want at 2 AM on a Monday morning, including recordings of Louis Farrakhan saying off-brand shit about the Jews, and it wouldn't be an issue, because while radio stations are required by law to abide by FCC guidelines, they only get in trouble with the FCC if someone listening in files a complaint. The FCC has the technology and the infrastructure to record every single thing that's aired on terrestrial radio. I mean if the NSA can record and save copies of our phone calls and emails for posterity, which they do, according to the documents leaked by Eric Snowden, but why should they bother? They don't have to sweat radio stations playing anything with subversive political content, because radio stations only play garbage music that appeals to the lowest common denominator.

If it occurred to anyone with The Combat Jack Show that a radio station might have a certain obligation to the city it's broadcast from, to play artists from that city, or that major labels might have some convoluted system in which they compensate stations like Hot 97 for playing their artists, they weren't about to ask. There was a lot of talk at the time about the song "All Gold Everything" by Trinidad James, which of course was big on Hot 97. This might have led to discussion of whether or not it's appropriate for a station like Hot 97 to propagate certain images of black people, whether they're excessively violent, or in this case, excessively coon-ish. Needless to say, I was no fan of "All Gold Everything," but generally speaking, I'm not in the business of telling people what they're allowed to do. Hot 97 shouldn't have played "All Gold Everything" so much because there's just plain not a lot to it; it's just some guy mumbling ignorant shit about doing drugs, his jewelry and what have you for four or five minutes straight. In fact, I suspect that that's why Trinidad James' major label career didn't even last long enough for him to release an album. As I discuss in my third book, NaS Lost, it's usually artists who can rhyme who have longevity in hip-hop, e.g. Nas, Jay, Eminem, LL, and even to a certain degree Lil Wayne.

Towards the end of the show, once it was clear that this was what's known in therapy culture as a safe space, Combat asked Ebro if he could have his own show on Hot 97. I guess you kinda gotta ask for your own show, right, if you're running a fake radio show and you have the guy who's responsible for giving people their own real radio shows on as a guest? Worst case scenario, he just says no. It's the same thought process behind trying to score with girls who hang out in night clubs alone and/or the lottery: you gotta play to win!

Ebro's actual response was something along the lines of, "You don't want a show on Hot 97," with the idea perhaps being that jobs in radio, unless you're Howard Stern or someone, pay less than you'd think; it's not like a podcast, in that you're not allowed to play the songs you want to play or discuss the things you'd like to discuss, you're basically just there to do as you're told by the Illuminati; and everyone will hate you and you'll be at constant risk of someone attacking you in public for playing such garbage music and not playing their song on the radio.

Really, if there was a way that you could make a comparable income from podcasting, you'd much rather just do a podcast. The key might be to figure out a way to charge payola to play certain songs, whether it's from major labels, or from drug dealers pretending to be rappers and CEOs of entertainment companies, like a lot of the artist-submitted content on World Star. Because podcasts aren't ostensibly publicly owned, like terrestrial radio, I don't see why it would be an issue legally. It might be necessary to disclose that you've been paid to promote something, but it seems like my TL on Instagram these days is filled with pictures of things people have been paid to promote—or given for free, which is the same as being paid to promote something—that aren't properly labeled as advertisements. If the government is enforcing that law at all, they're not doing a very good job of it. I don't want to buy something because I saw that someone else on the Internets bought it, not because I actually wanted it, and come to find out, they didn't even buy it. They got theirs for free. They don't even like that shit!

Then there was also the fact that Combat had spent the past few weeks trolling Ebro on Twitter, not to mention the fact that Peter Rosenberg once threatened to slap him in front of his kids. What was the likelihood, really, that Ebro would so much as consider hiring Combat Jack, without Peter Rosenberg pulling him aside and telling him not to, the same way Rosenberg's cousin Paul Rosenberg put Combat's career on hold at Sirius XM? That's what they do. (By "they" I mean the Rosenberg family.)

Hot 97 didn't need anymore black people anyway.

At that point, an ill-conceived campaign to rebrand the station as, essentially, the hip-hop station for white people, rather than "Where Hip-Hop Lives," was well underway. This may have been prompted by the fact that the newly ascendant Power 105, spurred by the success of The Breakfast Club, with Angela Yee and Charlamagne Tha God, was already gaining on Hot 97 in the ratings and would eventually overtake it. The Breakfast Club isn't exactly the voice of the hood, but it's a decidedly blacker show than Hot 97's morning show, which at the time was hosted by Peter Rosenberg, Cipha Sounds and Ebro—a Jewish guy, a Puerto Rican and a Jewish Halfrican American.

Fewer and fewer black people live in New York now, due to the rising price of real estate and things like gentrification and stop and frisk, all of which of course go hand in hand, and execs at Hot 97 may have felt that a whiter image for the station would only become more and more appropriate. White people, generally speaking, can't stand rap music made by other white people (with a few exceptions, natch), but they don't seem to mind hip-hop journalism written by white people, and hosting a radio show is kinda like journalism, right? In fact, it seems like more and more hip-hop journalism is taking on the form of podcasts, live interview series and what have you.

I didn't watch a single episode of the VH1 series This Is Hot 97, nor did very many people, if its abysmal ratings and quick cancellation were any indication, but the promos for it looked very... shall we say, multicultural. They looked like a Gap ad for a new line of denim for middle-age Hispanics, you know with a shorter inseam, and other assorted individuals of indeterminate ethnic origin. If you don't count Rosenberg, there wasn't an according to Hoyle white guy in the bunch, but there was only one black guy, Funkmaster Flex, who gave off a token-ish vibe, like the one black guy on a season of The Real World, who ends up arguing in the street with a Midwestern (read mildly racist) white chick about whether or not black people can be racist. If only there had been a similar scene on This Is Hot 97, in which Funkmaster Flex told Peter Rosenberg how he really felt about the fact that Rosenberg is hardly any better a DJ than someone who wanders into a Guitar Center off the street having never touched a turntable a day in his life, it might have saved the series.

The failure of This Is Hot 97, and the concurrent rise of Power 105, kicked off a series of unfortunate, embarrassing personnel changes, exacerbated by DJ Mister Cee's continual arrests for propositioning tranny hookers. Mister Cee, whose throwback mixes and tributes to dead rappers I have enjoyed, and who deejayed for legends like Big Daddy Kane and Biggie Smalls, and who's reportedly still eating off of Biggie's first LP, should have been the first person—or rather, the first major on-air personality of the bunch—to be let go, the first time he got caught trying to get a guy dressed as a girl to slob on his knob like corn on the cob. Not that there's necessarily anything wrong with that, if that's what you're into (I'm not), but it is illegal, and when he got busted that shit was all over the media. And lest we forget, the first time we heard about him getting caught wasn't the first time he got busted; it was just the first time someone down at the precinct recognized him from the booklet from Big Daddy Kane's second album, It's a Big Daddy Thing, where he's listed as the Nasty African, or N.A. for short. Ironically, that album is now mostly famous for the song "Pimpin' Ain't Easy," with the lines, "The Big Daddy law is anti-faggot / That means no homosexuality." Uh, thanks for clarifying! Arguably, this was the first use of the phrase "no homo" on a rap song, a good half a decade before that Red Hot Lover Tone album.

What kind of brother do you know who has a job where he can commit some sort of ridiculous crime, have it be all in the news, and continue showing up for work every day, as the face of the company (er, one of the faces of the company), with his boss ensuring him, in public, that there's nothing wrong with his lifestyle? I can hardly show up to work still drunk from the night before without having to sweat my boss calling me back to the office to sign a few papers, including one in which it's explained that I'm no longer allowed on the premises—and my job doesn't even involve interacting with the general public. The mop could care less if I'm drunk! Mister Cee had the ultimate in job security, because there was no way they could fire him without the gay community throwing a bitchfit and possibly threatening to boycott Hot 97's sponsors. Cee might have also tried to sue Hot 97 for discrimination, which to me is ridiculous, because he committed a crime, and that alone should be enough for him to have to leave, but I guess then the question becomes, has anyone else at Hot 97 been arrested? And what's the likelihood, really, that someone at a hip-hop radio station hasn't been arrested, even a station full of wannabes like Hot 97? It's a known fact that Funkmaster Flex puts a shoe on a woman on the reg. His baby's mother had to take out a restraining order.

For a period of time, there was a black chick who was co-hosting the morning show with Cipha Sounds and Rosenberg. She disappeared all of a sudden, and the next thing you know, Ebro, who was then just the program director, started co-hosting. Combat Jack, on the Ebro episode of The Combat Jack Show, asked him what happened to the black chick, and Ebro said she wanted to go live in Florida… which sounds like something you tell a little kid when his dog dies. "She went to live on a farm upstate." Combat was just like, "Oh, okay." Hopefully, she really did move down to Florida and get a job on the radio there, maybe with DJ Khaled. Has anyone heard from her since? Sometimes serial killers are able to prey on black women for years because no one thinks to report them missing, or if they do, everyone just assumes she was out there selling ass. As was the case with the assassinations of 2Pac and Biggie Smalls, it took Nick Broomfield to come over here and crack the case on one of history's most prolific killers of black women, this guy the Grim Sleeper, who may have killed as many as 100 black chicks. Black Girls' Lives Matter. Also, Black Girls Rock, though admittedly, I can't see that hashtag on Twitter and not think of "Some Girls." I'm part of the problem.

Because there were now three guys hosting the morning show, all in their 30s, all more or less the same height, and having a Halfrican American guy and a Puerto Rican guy was kinda redundant, at least in terms of skin tone, Ebro ended up getting rid of Cipha Sounds. Or rather, whoever had the authority to get rid of Cipha Sounds got rid of Cipha Sounds. Ebro hasn't been program director for a minute, having been given the opportunity, he says, to choose between continuing to be program director and co-hosting the morning show. For a while there, he was doing both. Before he left, Cipha Sounds had been reduced to a "glorified mixer," which I took to mean that he wasn't allowed to say anything. They may have even cut his mic off, like the Jeremy Glick episode of the O'Reilly Factor. That must have been difficult. He was replaced by a Hispanic girl who, while not unattractive, looks like she could be someone's mom, which makes me wonder why every segment involving her has to do with how hot she is. Maybe they can't think of anything else for her to say.

Cipha Sounds ended up taking the afternoon slot from Angie Martinez, who was poached by Power 105. A grizzled New York radio veteran, who'd been with Hot 97 for three decades, Martinez was considered "the voice of Hot 97." It didn't make sense why Hot 97 would want to get rid of her, or let Power 105 lure her away, except that she was kinda ethnic sounding, and maybe they were looking to take the station in a different direction.

A few months later, Mister Cee quit all of a sudden. He'd quit once before, after his third arrest (count 'em) for soliciting a tranny hooker, only to be convinced to reconsider by Ebro, after a bizarre, tearful on-air come to Jesus moment. This time, he just kinda up and disappeared, abruptly announcing his resignation via Twitter, after having been there for 21 years. Word on the street is that he was about to be let go anyway, and he decided he'd rather just quit. You can't sign up for unemployment if you just quit, right? I guess that's not as much of an issue for (minor) celebrity DJs.

Cipha Sounds' stint as Angie Martinez's replacement came to an abrupt halt when he complained publicly that the station seemed to be giving him the runaround. They gave him that afternoon slot as if they'd let him have it permanently, but he must have realized at some point that they were just stringing him along until they could find a permanent replacement for Angie Martinez. He aired his grievances on a podcast, and as I recall, he was gone by noon the next day. The station issued a press release stating that he didn't work there anymore, and uh, hopefully he can find a job somewhere else. Maybe he can drive an Uber. He'd been at the station for 17 years.

He was replaced in that afternoon time slot by a girl named Nessa, who'd been on a station in Ebro's native Bay Area and hosted something called the Girl Code on MTV. She sorta kinda resembles a girl named Tehmeena Afzal, who works for a car dealership in New York and takes a lot of sports-themed pictures in various states of undress. If her show had a visual, rather than just an audio, component, and it involved her leaning against a late-model Nissan while a guy just off camera sprayed her down with a water hose, like the real Tehmeena Afzal, and if it were available via the Internets, I might tune in.

09.

Touch My Body

"I don't know if they fags or what / Search a nigga down, and grabbing his nuts."

— Ice Cube

Word on the street is that Eric Garner was sexually assaulted by the NYPD, and that's what led to the interaction in which he was choked to death on a Staten Island sidewalk. He'd filed a formal complaint against the police, and they were there to harass him in retaliation.

If you plan to file a complaint against the police, your best bet is to skip town first and then file a complaint. If you rat out a cop and then just go about your regular routine, you can pretty much count on them harassing you, if not killing you.

Obviously, they could give a rat's ass about the consequences of being charged with harassment, if it didn't prevent them from harassing you in the first place. And why should they? On the rare occasion when a cop is found to have harassed someone, the city just pays out a settlement and the cop gets to keep his job.

Meanwhile, you can hardly drop a box of fluorescent light bulbs at Hardee's and keep your job. Light bulbs matter, it seems. Black lives? Not so much.

It's been alleged that a cop gave Eric Garner the ol' finger-in-the-culo once on a sidewalk while people walked by and could see him standing there with his pants down, with a cop's finger in his ass. In addition to any injury that resulted from having someone's finger in his ass, which I'm sure is uncomfortable, there was the embarrassment of people having to see him get violated in that way.

Eric Garner's family lived in Staten Island. Imagine if one of his kids walked by and saw him bent over on a sidewalk with a cop's finger in his ass.

They'd never be able to look at him the same way ever again. A daughter might have been at risk of ending up on a pole, if not a track. A son would have feared the police anyway, but still.

If I just had to have a cop stick a finger in my ass, because he had probable cause to believe that I might have some drugs shoved up my ass (which it seems like he should have to, per the Constitution), I would want it to be a female cop. And even then I would want it to be in private, in a room with the lights dimmed and some Luther Vandross playing in the background.

And then it would be my turn to check her for contraband. Possibly using more than just my finger. LOL

I'm assuming the cop who went knuckles deep on Eric Garner at least had on gloves. As sadistic as cops can be, no one wants to run the risk of getting mud caked beneath their fingernail. People in New York travel by foot a lot more often than we do out here in the flyover states, and I can only imagine the severity of the batwings situation. The fact that a cop would even subject himself to some shit like that just goes to show their commitment to trolling black people.

Daniel Pantaleo, a/k/a Guido the Killer Cop, the guy who choked out Eric Garner, has been accused of reaching down in perps' pants to play with their peens (see what I did there?) and making people strip naked in the street, to see if they've got any crack tucked beneath their ballsacks or whatever.

I'm sure these are all guys we're talking about, by the way. If it had been a woman, some feminist blog would have long since intervened, if not because of the indignity and the injustice of such harassment, then because some guy happened along as it was happening, took a pic with his cell phone, and posted it on Reddit.

At any rate, the NYPD had already paid out two settlements on Pantaleo's behalf before he choked out Eric Garner.

It isn't clear whether or not Pantaleo had ever played with Eric Garner's balls. They definitely seemed to know each other. In the video, Eric Garner tells Pantaleo that he's not dealing with this shit today, which suggests to me that he had to deal with shit like that most other days.

Part of Eric Garner's reluctance to submit to an arrest may have had to do with the fact that he hadn't committed a crime. That's usually one of the main reasons I don't want to go to jail. He'd been arrested for selling loose cigarettes on multiple occasions, but he didn't have any cigarettes on him that day.

Neither Pantaleo nor any of the rest of the cops on the scene thought to bring a pack of cigarettes—ideally something black people smoke like Newport or Salem—in case they accidentally killed him and it turned out he wasn't even selling loose cigarettes. Some cops carry an extra gun, known as a ham sandwich, to plant on perps they accidentally shoot.

The cops arrived on the scene in the first place because there had been reports of a fight, which Garner supposedly broke up. Hindsight being 20/20, he should have turned and walked the other way, which is what I do in 100% of situations in which I see people gathered to do something wrong and about 95% of situations in which I see people gathered to do something right. If enough people are around, something bad is bound to happen eventually. People suck.

Eric Garner was a better man than I am. He stuck around and broke up that fight, and he didn't bother to take off before the cops pulled up, likely because he figured he didn't have anything to worry about, since he hadn't committed a crime, right?

Wrong!

Garner wasn't involved in the fight, aside from having broken it up, and he didn't have any contraband on him, but the cops were gonna arrest him anyway, because why not. If he really didn't do anything wrong, he could explain that to the judge, and the judge would probably let him go home. As the saying goes, you can beat the rap but you can't beat the ride.

The worst part of the Eric Garner snuff footage isn't the part where they finally choke the life out of him, which is difficult to discern from the way the video is shot, it's the part where he complains about how often he's harassed by the police. You can tell from the sound of his voice that he'd been deeply traumatized. He'd already been killed, in a sense. This was just a matter of removing his body.

———————————

The NYPD killed Eric Garner again, metaphorically speaking, when it was announced that a grand jury somehow decided not to indict Guido the Killer Cop, this despite the fact that cops in New York aren't allowed to use chokeholds, let alone the fact that they didn't have a good reason to arrest Eric Garner in the first place.

Not to mention the fact that it was all caught on tape, and anyone who saw it—which was pretty much anyone who watched the news at any point in the late summer of 2K14—could see that this was some ol' bullshit.

Even George W. Bush, asked about the grand jury decision in an interview, was like, I can't even believe that shit.

This was maybe 10 days after the verdict in the Mike Brown case and the subsequent rioting in Ferguson, so it wasn't a complete surprise. I'm not sure what would have been, at that point. Maybe if Eric Garner's family had to pay Guido the Killer Cop for hurting his wrist.

It's not unheard of for a suspect to be charged with ruining a cop's uniform after he's been beaten to a bloody pulp, but I think they only pull that shit in cases where the guy doesn't die.

The cop's already getting away with murder, I'm sure they figured—they didn't want people to get too upset.

New York Mayor Bill de Blasio, in an address intended to keep black people from burning down New York like they did Ferguson, expressed sympathy with the Black Lives Matter movement. He explained how he has to tell his son Dante to watch out for the police—which seems pretty ridiculous when you think about it, given that he's the mayor, but I guess he hasn't been mayor for that long.

de Blasio is married to a black woman, who in the 1980s, wrote an article for Ebony magazine called "Why I'm a Lesbian," or something to that effect. But the mayor must have since brought her back amongst the heterosexual with the strength of his pipe game. Their son Dante has a ginormous afro, which is probably for the best: that way, the cops know not to put a shoe on him, lest the mayor have them fired, if that's even possible.

If I were in New York and I looked anything like Dante de Blasio, I might grow a ginormous afro just so the police would think I was the mayor's son. I'd be getting away with all kinds of shit!

The NYPD already didn't fuxwit Bill de Blasio, because he got rid of stop and frisk.

Stop and frisk was the program in which, if the cops saw a black guy on the

street between the ages of 8 and 80 (babies and the extreme elderly were ex-
empted), they'd harass him for no apparent reason. The idea was that the guy
might have a gun on him, and this would help cut down on shootings.

Typically, best case scenario, he'd have a little weed in his pocket, which
either isn't illegal in New York or it's decriminalized. I know you're allowed
to have it on you, you just can't have it out in the open, but cops were tricking
people into bringing it out in the open by asking them to empty their pockets.

Legally, they were supposed to go after other races of people and women as
well, but they found it easiest to just stick with black guys, because no one would
have a hard time believing that a black guy was doing something illegal anyway, as demonstrated by the fact that people still try to argue that Eric Garner
wouldn't have been choked to death if he hadn't been selling loose cigarettes.

de Blasio campaigned on getting rid of stop and frisk, on the basis that it
was both racist and retarded, but he may have ended up having to get rid of
it regardless of whether or not he wanted to, in part because the NYPD was
quite literally running out of dreaded n-words to arrest, and in part because the
city was having to pay money out the ass to people who got their asses kicked
for no apparent reason or their balls played with.

The only way stop and frisk would have been able to continue was if they
raised taxes so that the city would have enough money for the resulting civ-
il-rights lawsuit payouts, and simple logic would dictate that people wouldn't
be willing to pay more in taxes to subsidize police brutality—though not necessarily because they believe that black lives matter.

The whole purpose of police brutality, aside from amusing the police, is to
saddle people with fines to fund the city government, so that they don't have
to raise taxes. Raising taxes to pay for the police to harass people, in that sense,
would be the very definition of hustling backwards.

Also, lest we forget, the NYPD is deeply racist. In the weeks following Eric
Garner's death, when people began to show up to protests wearing shirts that
said I Can't Breathe and holding signs that said Black Lives Matter, the cops
trolled them by holding their own protests, where they wore shirts that said I
Can Breathe and held signs that said All Lives Matter, among other things.

It's likely that many members of the NYPD would have disliked Bill de
Blasio even if he hadn't ended stop and frisk, for the same reason the teabag-

gers went all batshit the summer after Obama took office, in '09. de Blasio himself isn't black, but his family is. There's one and a half black people living in Gracie Mansion, and who knows what they're doing in there. They might be in there frying fish.

A few weeks after the Eric Garner verdict was announced, some nutjob came up to New York from Baltimore and killed a couple of cops. I think he also shot his girlfriend in Baltimore, but that went almost completely unpublicized, which is highly ironic in light of the Black Lives Matter protests.

Ismaaiyl Brinsley, or whatever the guy's name was, announced on social media that he was coming to New York to kill the police, long before he got here. Not to be insensitive about this, but the fact that they couldn't stop him before he got there, or prevent him from killing those two cops once he did, is a testament to their ineptitude.

Or it may have just been a matter of where he decided to strike. I've heard that in parts of New York, near where the new World Trade Center is and other Illuminati strongholds, not only are you constantly being filmed anywhere you can possibly go in public but they're also recording your voice, if you say anything, and storing it for posterity.

Theoretically, they can take a picture of you when you arrive there, cross reference it with a database of terrorists and other people who don't have any business being there, and have a cop's hand down your pants with a quickness. I've heard stories of people being stopped by the police in parts of Manhattan and the cops don't even bother to ask for ID, because they already know who you are.

Would it have been possible to roll up on two cops sitting in a cruiser parked outside the new World Trade Center having a donut, if that's possible, and pop numerous caps in their asses? I'm gonna guess that it wouldn't have been. Your best bet is to focus on areas where black people live, where I'm sure surveillance, if not police presence, is a lot more lax.

The two cops Brinsley killed weren't white. One was a Hispanic guy and one was Asian. You'd think he might try to find a couple of white cops, given the extent to which this incident has been racialized, but maybe that's not giving the guy enough credit. He may have been a crazed cop killer, but he was no racist.

I'd say that's something for racists to think about.

Speaking of which, the NYPD made a big show of turning their backs to Mayor de Blasio at services for the slain cops. Which is kinda silly, if you think about it. I'm sure the cops' families were in enough pain without their fellow officers trying to turn this into some sort of political statement, when in reality they're probably just pissed off that they aren't able to milk the city for overtime like they could during stop and frisk.

Based on what little I know about Bill de Blasio, including the fact that he used to be a pothead and apparently he's got a taste for brown sugar, he seems like a chill bro. I wonder if he would even give a shit, on a personal level, if the police turned their backs to him. What pothead do you know who would be upset at the police not looking at them?

If anything, he might not like being disrespected in public like that. One of the things racist white people try to do to black politicians—or in this case chill white politicians married to black women—is disrespect them in public. Barack Obama had to fire a general for talking shit about him in Rolling Stone. If he'd had that chick from Arizona who waved a finger in his face killed, it would have been too obvious.

Because seemingly the entire NYPD turned their backs to Bill de Blasio, or all the cops who showed up to this event, he couldn't just fire them all. One thing he might have considered is just getting rid of five of them at random, if he's allowed to do that. That would have sent out a message, and it would have put the rest of them in fear that the same thing might happen to them. They're already not getting as much overtime.

In the weeks following the funerals for the two cops who got killed, continuing into 2015, the NYPD just stopped doing their jobs. They stopped putting parking tickets on cars and stopped arresting people for things like having an open container of alcohol in public. You could leave your car pretty much anywhere in New York and not have to sweat getting a ticket or having it towed. A few people actually tried it and got away with it.

It would have been as good a time as ever to spend a weekend in the city, walking around getting wasted, leaving your car wherever and taking a piss whenever you felt the need, as if you were in St. Louis.

It was announced that the police would be making arrests "only when they had to," which, as many a commentator pointed out, meant that they normally arrest people that they don't have to arrest. Apparently, a lot of people. The overall number of arrests dropped by a full two-thirds, while the number of arrests for BS quality of life offenses dropped by upwards of 100%. Does that mean we can get rid of two-thirds of the police and it might actually make us safer? Probably.

Eventually, the NYPD just kinda went back to work without any major concessions from de Blasio that I'm aware of, and I'm thinking this is because they understood on a certain level that they serve no real purpose. Cutting off parking tickets for a few weeks may have cost the city a few dollars, but it's not like they rely on traffic fines for damn near their entire budget, like some of the municipalities near where I live. Cops' jobs don't matter as much as they'd like to think.

———————

A few days after the Eric Garner video hit the Internets, Spike Lee had one of the guys who edits his films take that video and edit in clips from the scene in Do the Right Thing in which Radio Raheem is choked out by the NYPD, as if it wasn't already clear how similar those scenes were.

Maybe some people did need reminding. After all, it had been a quarter of a century. (Yikes!) In fact, when Eric Garner died, it was almost 25 years to the day after Do the Right Thing premiered. That summer, there was a big block party near where the movie was filmed, in Brooklyn, to celebrate.

In an interview to promote his most recent film as of this writing, the crowdfunded Da Sweet Blood of Jesus, someone asked Spike Lee if he'd make a movie about the death of Eric Garner. He was like, fuck that shit! Someone else would have to make that movie, he said.

He didn't elaborate further, but you got the sense that he wouldn't have been interested in doing something so similar to Do the Right Thing. Arguably, Do the Right Thing is his best film (I'm partial to Malcolm X), and white people seem to fuxwit it a lot more than they did when it was released back in the late '80s, when there was fear it might cause riots. It regularly appears on lists of the best films of all time. Any sequel Spike could make at this point almost certainly wouldn't be as well received, and I don't know if there's really that much more to say on the topic. He's already been there and done that.

Mookie, Spike Lee's character in Do the Right Thing, appears in Red Hook
Summer, released in 2012, a truly awful film. He's done a lot of movies people
don't like, and even more movies people didn't see, but Red Hook Summer
might be the one Spike Lee movie (ahem, joint) I saw that I thought was truly
bad. Granted, it's the screenplay that sinks it, not so much Spike Lee's direction, or the actors, but I'm assuming he was the one who decided this screenplay was worthy of being filmed. Either he couldn't tell it wasn't any good,
or maybe he couldn't afford to have someone else polish it up some, with the
small budget they were working with. I would have been more than happy to
take a pass at it. I know Jack Schitt about writing a movie, but almost anything
you could have done to that movie would have made it better. I could have
added a sex scene. Not involving the kids, obvs.

Oldboy is the one Spike Lee joint that's not in fact A Spike Lee Joint. Spike
had the studio that released the film remove that designation from the film's
title sequence because he was upset with changes they forced him to make. It's
not clear how the version of Oldboy you can pull up on Netflix differs from the
one he originally envisioned, and I couldn't find any information on what he
had to cut, after having spent as much time as I was willing to spend trying to
look it up on the Internets. Oldboy is plenty violent by American garbage mall
movie standards, and it's got some gross sex shit in it. I won't ruin it for anyone
who might still be interested in seeing it, other than to say that I really didn't
need to see that. Otherwise, I didn't find it to be such a tragedy. Call me crazy.

It's quite possible that Spike Lee has arrived at a point in his career in
which he can't get a film made unless it's some bullshit sports documentary
as part of ESPN's 30 for 30 series—essentially just old sports footage edited
together with talking heads describing the sports footage you just saw. Even
then, I'm sure they'd have him on a short leash. You know they don't play that
shit at ESPN. A Spike Lee joint on the Ray Rice elevator video would be out
of the question, as interesting as that would be. The last time Spike was involved in legit Hollywood commercial fare was Oldboy, and that seems to have
had the exact opposite of its intended effect.

Da Sweet Blood of Jesus was funded via Kickstarter. I actually kicked in a
dollar myself. In the video Spike posted soliciting donations, he promised on
his dead mother's grave that every single dollar raised via Kickstarter would

end up on the screen, and that he wasn't taking a fee to direct the film. I'm not sure what form the dollar I donated took. Maybe Spike used it to cop a coffee at White Castle on the way to the set, if they haven't gone up in price. They were $0.89 when I was there, back in the early '00s, but I remember they went up during my time there.

I don't make enough money to justify donating any money at all to someone's Kickstarter, but sometimes I like to drop a dollar on a Kickstarter anyway, if it looks like it might be interesting. That dollar alone won't help much, but you can post on Facebook, Twitter, etc. that you chipped in, and maybe other people will donate. If you can get enough people to kick in just a dollar, Sally Struthers might argue, you don't have to sweat copping one of the BS high-dollar-amount packages that come with a shoutout on Twitter and a DVD that cost like $0.79 to make. You can't even get a cup of coffee at White Castle for $0.79!

Spike did receive some criticism for trying to get broke individuals like me to help him fund his movie, when apparently he lives in a house that's worth $30 million. He's directed films for 30 some-odd years now, and a few of them even turned a profit, but he's also married to a girl who comes from the Brahmin class of negroes. I think her father was an executive at a large corporation or something to that effect. Combat Jack, who seeks to cultivate relationships with people who have a lot of money, used to hit that back in the day. He left it wet for Spike. If Spike is aware of this, it didn't come up during the Spike Lee episode of the Combat Jack Show, the fact that they're Eskimo brothers and all.

Ironically, the release of Da Sweet Blood of Jesus coincided with a hot period (no pun intended) for black film... which is something that happens every now and again. Once, for example, in the early 2000s, Denzel Washington and Halle Berry both won the top acting statues at the Academy Awards, and I think they may have also given Sidney Poitier a lifetime achievement award at the same ceremony. They do that sometimes, and then they don't give another black filmmaker an award, or maybe even a decent job, for like 10 years.

Da Sweet Blood of Jesus was released via video on demand in early 2K15. I think you could pay like $5 and watch it on your computer. I didn't bother, because I wasn't about to spend any more money after I already kicked in that dollar. Arguably, the price of my viewing should have been prorated.

Around the exact same time, a show called Empire hit the air. Apparently, it's some sort of prime-time soap opera loosely based on the mid '90s hip-hop scene. The great Terrence Howard plays one of the leads and says he based his character in part on Suge Knight. I've also heard it described as a quasi-sequel to Hustle and Flow, which definitely makes me interested to see it. Taraji P. Henson, who played one of the hoo-ers in Hustle and Flow, is the female lead in Empire.

Empire came on as a midseason replacement, with its first season running 12 episodes. Its audience grew each week, and by the end of that first season it was the most popular show on TV, ahead of The Big Bang Theory. (Wow!) The finale was the most-watched season finale of a new series in 10 years, which is quite a feat given that people don't really watch network series anymore. The credits had hardly finished rolling on that last episode when a site called Deadline Hollywood ran an article about how there might be too many black people on TV.

There weren't many black shows on TV other than Empire, but Empire hit the air during pilot season, and when the TIs saw how many people were tuning in they started casting black actors in a lot of their pilots, including shows that didn't have shit to do with black people. A pilot, as explained in Pulp Fiction, is an episode of a show they shoot to show to execs to decide if it should become a series. In other words, black actors hadn't been given jobs, they'd just been allowed to interview, and already it was becoming "an issue."

Empire was produced and co-created by Lee Daniels, who directed Precious and The Butler, two of the black community's finest moments on film in recent years. I kinda liked Precious, but The Butler was just awful. It was almost like Lee Daniels and the studio were trolling us. It's like a parody that you might see as a film within a film, like the film in which Ben Stiller's character in Tropic Thunder went full retard. But both Precious and The Butler made boatloads of money. The Butler became one of the very few black-directed films to gross over $100 million.

Mo'Nique won an Academy Award for her role in Precious, but she says she's since been blackballed by Lee Daniels. She hasn't really done shit since then. Daniels, for his part, says she was being disruptive during the awards-season process. She tried to get the studio to pay her extra money to go around and do interviews, to campaign for the awards she ended up winning. She was only paid $50,000 to appear in the film, which grossed over $60 million on a budget of $10 million, and I'm sure they made more money as a result of her winning that Oscar.

In late 2K14, Kim Jong-Un, pissed about the Seth Rogen movie The Interview, hacked into the email system at Sony Pictures. Content of the emails began to appear on the Internets. Among other things that were revealed were that the white lady who ran Sony Pictures joked with a white guy who worked there about Barack Obama probably liking Django Unchained, and that they threatened to purposely sabotage one of Kevin Hart's films because he tried to get the studio to pay him to promote a film on Twitter, which is a fairly common thing these days.

On CNN to promote Empire, Lee Daniels was asked by Don Lemon if he'd blackballed Mo'Nique. He said she blackballed herself with the demands she made during the awards campaign for Precious, and then by having the sheer balls to not thank the studio when she accepted her Oscar. It's important, he said, to "play ball" with the TIs, lest you end up unemployable. Lemon said that some people consider that selling out. "Well, I guess I'm a sellout then," Daniels responded, "but I'm not about to not work. [...] I'll see you in the theaters!"

10.
Runaway Slave Master

"Dear Diary, The ass was fat."
    — Arthur Read

Hot 97's Summer Jam has a separate stage off in the parking lot for up and coming artists and underground groups. The idea, supposedly, is that this smaller stage is for artists who might one day play the larger stage, in the actual stadium.

You never hear anything about this smaller stage. Sometimes you see videos of things that take place in the parking lot at Summer Jam—which I'm thinking must be somewhere near this smaller stage—on World Star. You'd think they'd be fight videos, with this being World Star and with Summer Jam being a rap concert, but they're usually just videos of people being sexually inappropriate.

There's always a lot of girls walking around in street-walker outfits, and they're always ginormous black and Hispanic women who appear to be in their 30s and 40s, though they could be as young as middle school age, who knows. If you notice, many of them have short arms and are kinda permanently tilted forward at the waist like a T Rex.

I've seen multiple videos of girls giving guys "sloppy top" behind cars while other people stand around and watch, and even videos of couples "getting it in," right out there in the open, plus a video of some tick-like hoodrat walking around with her ass hanging out of her pants, being followed by 10 or 15 guys, clearly enjoying the attention. A supermodel could have walked by, and those guys wouldn't have given a shit. It's a different aesthetic ideal they're after at Summer Jam.

If I ever attended Summer Jam, like if I were in NY and I lost a bet or something, I can't tell you that I'd go inside. It seems like there's a lot more interesting things going on in the parking lot, plus there's that underground stage. If there's any good rap music at Summer Jam at all, it would have to be on that underground stage. Inside at Summer Jam 2K14, you'll recall, was G-Unit, Iggy Azalea, Nicki Minaj and Childish Gambino.

Nicki Minaj, by then, had either been there, or had been scheduled to be there, for three years in a row. She was the scheduled headliner in 2K12 and had to pull out at the last minute, like Peter Rosenberg's father, over some shit Rosenberg said on the underground stage. The next year, the TIs arranged for them to kiss and make up on air, and she made a brief cameo appearance at Summer Jam 2K13 during a set by 2 Chainz, who has a song about how all he wants for his birthday is a big booty ho. Note that Summer Jam wasn't actually on his birthday.

In 2012, Rosenberg told fans assembled before the parking lot stage that he knew some of them were girls who were there to sing along with "Starships" later that evening, because why else would a girl be at a rap concert, but fuck that bullshit, they were about to listen to some real hip-hop!

Unbeknownst to Rosenberg, there was a live feed of this playing on Nicki Minaj's website. Who even knew that Nicki Minaj had a website, let alone that it would be running a live feed of the parking lot stage at Summer Jam? What sense does that make? Artist websites seem like a relic of the time when you'd go to the actual Space Jam website to find out more about, erm, the movie Space Jam. In fact, the Space Jam website is still online to this day and does not appear to have been updated since 1996.

Apparently, Nicki Minaj has a large community of fans who all coalesce around this site, not unlike Lady Gaga's Little Monsters or Justin Bieber's Beliebers, or the legions of sad, deranged hoodrats who troll sites like Twitter and Tumblr for any mention of Beyoncé and would probably defend her quite literally to the death—which is the name of an M.O.P. they've never heard of, this despite the fact that M.O.P. did that song with LFO. Anyone who takes Beyoncé seriously as a musician is too young to remember LFO. One of those guys is dead now. Another one is seriously damaged from being effed in the a both literally and figuratively by Lou Pearlman. There was an episode of the

Stern Show about it, but you had to be listening live. They edited all of the sex stuff out of the reruns.

The Wu-Tang Clan had a group of Internets-based superfans in the '90s. They were called wiggers. LOL

One of Nicki Minaj's superfans, the Hoo-ers, saw Rosenberg talking shit about "Starships" on the parking lot stage and hit her up on Twitter. Shocked and appalled that Hot 97 would treat her with such disrespect, she canceled her performance. She probably wasn't getting paid shit anyway. The reason those radio station summer festival shows get such amazing lineups—or could if they wanted to, in this case—is because there's the implicit threat that if you don't agree to show up and play for free, or next to it, they'll stop playing your records and your career will be destroyed. From what I understand, Hot 97 didn't play Minaj's megahit "Starships" much anyway. It was a bridge too far for even Hot 97, which is saying something. Minaj is signed to Young Money, along with Lil Wayne, Drake, Tyga, etc., and that's all garbage commercial rap stations have played for the past five years or so, so I doubt they were at any real risk of retaliation. There's only a small handful of major label rappers with truly viable careers, at this point. Even Kanye's sales are in the toilet.

It's ironic that Nicki Minaj once had beef with Hot 97, given that Nicki Minaj is the quintessential Hot 97 artist. She started out as a grimy underground rapper, appearing in hood DVDs looking like Snoop from The Wire but with worse hair, talking about how Remy Ma ate the box, and then she signed to a major label and hit the big time with songs that many black people haven't heard to this day, and wouldn't want to anyway. She pretty much is Hot 97.

I heard of "Starships" for a while before I actually heard it. Sometimes a song can be the most popular song in the country for weeks on end and I won't hear it, because I don't listen to the radio or go to places where people would be listening to some shit like that.

I pulled up to a light once, in what was probably the summer of 2K12, and in the car next to me were three teenage white chicks singing "Starships" at the top of their lungs. I started to follow them around for a while just for, you know, anthropological purposes, but with technology these days they could have easily called the cops on me, and there's no way I would have been able to explain to them that I write about rap music on the Internets. They might have Mike Brown'd me on GP.

I drive a van.

———————

The problem with dominating the pop charts with garbage pop music is that it's not a very good long-term career strategy, because anyone can make garbage pop music.

Those songs are all written and produced by the Swedish, the same people who brought you ABBA (so clearly they know what they're doing), and I don't know that it matters who's singing. They've got technology that can make it sound like you can sing—it's what J. Lo used to use back in the late '90s. On an episode of some Ice-T reality show, he had a guy produce a pretty legit-sounding pop song by his wife Coco, just to prove how easy it is. With her ass, it might have gone to number one, if they officially released it. Remember, they're counting YouTube videos now at Billboard.

If Nicki Minaj had that much success with songs like "Starships" and "Super Bass," and she's a 30 some-odd year-old attitudinal former Red Lobster waitress with a sloppy tank ass, imagine the success we could have with a white chick, the Illuminati might have figured.

Enter Iggy Azalea.

A white female rapper from Australia, Iggy Azalea was signed to T.I. back when he was still famous enough to have random weed carriers assigned to him by his label. That was a few prison stints and garbage albums ago. Now he could almost be signed to her, if there were any way that could work or seem at all appropriate.

Acting as a black public cosigner is an increasingly popular late-career move for black musicians. It's a way to keep those checks rolling in when no one wants to buy your albums anymore. Usher donned a cape for Justin Bieber on TMZ, when they found that video of Bieber singing a song about the dreaded n-word. Hopefully he got paid a little extra that month.

Nelly raps on uber-popular country songs, including one that set some sort of Billboard record. And T.I. was on Robin Thicke's "Blurred Lines," which positively dominated the pop charts in 2K13. Both Nelly and T.I. may have banged Floyd Mayweather's baby's mother, and Mayweather may have returned the favor to T.I., leading T.I. to tempt fate by swinging on Mayweather.

That may have also been what happened between Floyd and Fiddy, leading Fiddy to mock Floyd for not being able to read. Floyd prefers to surround himself with a certain class of women, and as Strom Thurmond would say, it's been the bane of his existence.

To hear the wiki tell it, Iggy Azalea traveled to the US at 15, telling her parents she was going on a holiday (which is what they call vacations in Australia), and then just decided to stay, living in Miami, Houston and Atlanta. There's so much about that story that doesn't seem quite right, but I guess it could be true. Wikipedia is the world's most accurate encyclopedia, and Iggy Azalea is famous enough that someone would have noticed by now if it wasn't.

It doesn't make sense that her mom would just allow her to remain in the US, by herself, as a 15-year-old girl, except that her family was supposedly very poor and maybe her mom couldn't afford to come get her. I heard she cleaned hotel rooms for a living.

Which raises the question of how Iggy Azalea got here in the first place. People whose moms clean hotel rooms for a living don't go on random vacations halfway around the world. Unless some Arab guy from Instagram is footing the bill.

A Britney Spears-esque pop video that appeared and promptly disappeared from the Internets in 2K14, right during the height of Iggy Azalea mania, suggests that maybe she first came here to become the next Kylie Minogue, but some of the cities she was living in make me wonder if she didn't get caught up in "human trafficking."

Kool Keith, in an interview on The Combat Jack Show, said she used to work for Tim Dog back when Tim Dog—who was later the subject of an episode of Dateline about a gigolo scam he was running on older white women—was living in Atlanta. He said Tim Dog had her making him breakfast and going to get orange juice. Read into that what you will.

Iggy Azalea might still be fetching orange juice for middle-aged black men if it weren't for a surge in the popularity of black music performed by white artists. It was all anyone wanted to hear in 2K13, the year of "Blurred Lines," if the pop charts were any indication.

That year, for the first time since 1958, there wasn't a single song by a black artist that hit number one on the Hot 100. Less than 10 years prior, in 2004, it was the exact opposite. Not only was there not a song by a white artist that hit number one that year, there wasn't a song featuring a white artist. Pioneering white rapper Eminem was already on the journey up his own asshole that began with the release of Encore and therefore couldn't spit a hot 16.

The closest thing to a number one song by a white artist that year was "Lean Back" by Fat Joe (really it was by his weed carriers Terror Squad—credit where credit is due), who's Puerto Rican, which is a type of black person, per the one-drop rule, which is why they're allowed to use the dreaded n-word.

Iggy Azalea rode the wave of cultural appropriation right to the top of the pop charts (and hence to the bank) in 2K14, with the songs "Fancy," featuring Charli XCX, and Ariana Grande's "Problem," on which Azalea is featured.

Two things: (1) Ariana Grande sounds like something you can order at Taco Bell, and perhaps it should be (on the late-night menu, a/k/a Fourthmeal). (2) Ariana Grande's "Problem" sounds like the name of an adult film, back when adult films had classy titles.

Anyway, those songs weren't just popular, they were historically popular. At one point, "Fancy" was the number one song in the country and "Problem" was the number two song in the country. It was the first time an artist had done that with their first two (hit) singles since The Beatles.

Of course neither of those songs became so popular because people actually listened to them and decided they were the two most worthy songs on the radio at that particular moment.

"Problem" may have benefited from the fact that the artwork for its single might be the hottest artwork for a single since Carly Rae Jepsen's "Call Me Maybe" in 2K12, as briefly discussed in Infinite Crab Meats. It would have been even hotter if Iggy Azalea struck the same pose, because Ariana Grande has the body of a middle school-age girl, but the most important thing is that she doesn't appear to be wearing pants.

"Fancy" benefited from iHeartRadio's (a/k/a Clear Channel's) On the Verge program, in which each of its 840 stations here in the US was required to play it at least 150 times, at which point they were free to decide if they wanted to continue playing it... depending on whether or not it somehow became a hit.

People like songs that sound familiar, whether they're songs they've heard before or songs that merely seem familiar. The best songs sound familiar the first time you hear them—it's how you know it's a good song. Something similar happens with women. Hot chicks always seem to look familiar, and not just because there's a pron analogue for almost any attractive woman you could possibly find.

Producers have figured out how to make songs sound instantly familiar, not through the quality of the songwriting, but by wantonly ripping off hits of the past, e.g. "Blurred Lines," which cops the feel of Marvin Gaye's "Got to Give It Up" (nullus), and Sam Smith "Stay With Me," which has more or less the exact same melody as Tom Petty's "Won't Back Down."

"Fancy" was the fourth single released from Azalea's album, The New Classic (lol). None of the first three was part of the On the Verge program, and that's probably why they didn't catch on, despite their amazing videos. I took a look at several of her videos, both pre- and post-"Fancy," while "researching" this chapter. It took all the willpower I could muster to tear myself away. Wild horses were no match for dat ass.

Pre-"Fancy," Iggy Azalea was most famous for pics and videos of her ass. Tumblr was positively lousy with GIF images made from the videos for obscure pre-"Fancy" singles—or so I've been told.

There were also videos on World Star of her twerking on stage and encouraging fans to touch her ass. She'd arrange herself near the edge of the stage, bend over and let guys reach up and spank her. Attendance at her shows skyrocketed, I bet. At the time, I joked-not-joked about copping a ticket to an Iggy Azalea show just to touch her ass.

The week her album dropped, she went on the radio and complained about guys trying to fingerbang her. She said guys, who may have seen the same videos I saw, were hitting her up on Twitter to inform her that they'd be at the show and they were gonna try to go elbow deep, if possible, like at a Celebrity Skin-era Hole concert.

This led to many an article with a highly clickable headline, and it might have led to even more guys copping tickets to her shows, for fingerbanging purposes, never mind what she said on the radio. Iggy Azalea couldn't lose! Unless you count non-consensual fingerbanging as losing.

Towards the end of 2K13, after it became clear that no black artist would have a hit that year, but a few months still before the rise of Iggy Azalea, it was suggested that Nicki Minaj represented the black community's best hope of reclaiming the top of the pop charts in 2K14 and maybe our only hope period. "Starships" had been all over the radio in 2K12, though it never rose any higher than number five on the Hot 100.

Instead, Pharrell Williams became the first black artist to hit number one on the Hot 100 in over a year, with "Happy," a song no one really likes, and, like the Pharrell-produced "Blurred Lines," another Marvin Gaye ripoff. It may have been aided by a scam in which people were encouraged to watch its YouTube video for 24 hours straight, though it did arrive on the heels of both the Robin Thicke song and Daft Punk's Pharrell-featuring "Get Lucky."

Nicki Minaj's "Pills and Potions" never rose any higher than number 24. I don't recall ever hearing it, but I'm thinking it may have just been a "street single" intended to shore up her credibility after what Peter Rosenberg said about her at Summer Jam. If so, it just goes to show how far he threw her off of her game. What sense does it make for her to be concerned with her street cred, if she's going after the same kids who copped "Fancy?"

Nevertheless, Minaj was fêted at the 2K14 BET Awards, where there isn't a black celebrity so obscure that she can't be invited. In fact, the BET Awards' tendency to invite obscure black celebrities, who then trend briefly on Twitter, was the impetus for the creation of the term Black People Twitter, by yours truly. It eventually came to be known as Black Twitter, which I can't take any credit for, but I notice that the Black Twitter subreddit is still called r/Black-PeopleTwitter.

Incidentally, r/BlackPeopleTwitter was recently declared the most "problematic" subreddit on all of Reddit—which is saying something, if you know anything about Reddit—according to an algorithm that must just scan pages for "hate speech." But supposedly, r/BlackPeopleTwitter is run by black people, to spotlight the best of Black Twitter.

Accepting her BET Award, Nicki Minaj patted herself on the back, Barry Horowitz style, for writing her own rhymes, with the implication being that

Iggy Azalea, who'd been eating Nicki Minaj's lunch all summer long (no Remy Ma), didn't write the brilliant rhymes on songs like "Fancy."

T.I. has denied writing Azalea's lyrics, and that seems like it might be true. Her rhymes are worse than the rhymes he used to write for Lil Bow Wow, and they're not so good that she couldn't have written them herself. T.I. isn't listed as a songwriter in the album's credits as they appear in the wiki, which means that if he did write her rhymes he did it for an upfront fee rather than part of her publishing. You'd think he'd know better. Then again, this is T.I. we're talking about.

Nicki Minaj's next single, "Anaconda," definitely was intended to top the pop charts. You can tell from the artwork for its cover, which I'm sure (most) guys in prison would prefer even to the covers of Ariana Grande's "Problem" and Carly Rae Jepsen's "Call Me Maybe."

Minaj appears on the cover of the "Anaconda" single in a thong, in a squatting position, her back to the camera, her head turned so you can still see her face, like in pron. Her skin had been lightened and nasty rolls of fat had been removed from her stomach, while her ass was left in what appears to be more or less its natural state. Clearly, it was intended to be a reference to the posters for Lil Kim's Hard Core, from '96, arguably the GOAT female rap album, if we're not counting Fugees' The Score. Granted, I haven't heard very many other female rap albums.

Sensing an opportunity for some attention, Lil Kim struck back with "Identity Theft" which sounded as if it had been recorded on a laptop computer, though its cover—a picture of a driver's license with Lil Kim's personal information on it and Nicki Minaj's face—was amusing and surprisingly well put together. She might have just considered launching a Photoshop-only attack on Minaj, possibly via r/BlackPeopleTwitter.

White guys claim to be into ass now—in fact, 2K14 was called the Year of the Ass in some asinine think piece—but the "Anaconda" video may have been a bridge too far. White guys on Twitter seemed largely indifferent. Few seemed to participate in a meme called #TweetYourAnacondaVideoReaction that involved posting a pic or Vine suggesting that you were masturbating, along with that hashtag. White guys aren't big on hashtag games anyway.

Taylor Swift's "Shake It Off" hit the Internets the day before "Anaconda," in what may have been a matter of intentional counterprogramming, like when a Hollywood studio releases a rom-com the same weekend as a big action movie. Taylor Swift, for a number of reasons, is the anti-Nicki Minaj.

The "Shake It Off" video has girls twerking in its thumbnail image on YouTube, but otherwise it's the most sexless thing there ever was. You could probably get a more powerful rod watching the video for "Foolish Beat" by the legendarily unfapworthy Debbie Gibson (Bill Hicks wasn't a fan), which is a much better song—and I'll have you know, Debbie Gibson wrote and produced that song herself. She was the youngest person ever to write and produce a number one song. I don't know what happened to her career. She might have considered going bottomless.

Like Lorde's "Royals," another big black-sounding song by a white artist from 2K13, that halcyon year for musical caucasity, the "Shake It Off" video seems to criticize black culture as it's presented in rap videos. Also, Taylor Swift may have purposely worn "mom jeans," which make white chicks' asses look even worse than they would otherwise, to alienate a black audience, the way white pron chicks will avoid doing interracial scenes until late in their careers, after their bodies have already started to fall apart.

Earl Sweatshirt, ex-Odd Future member, announced on Twitter that he hadn't seen the "Shake It Off" video, but he found it offensive anyway. He said it perpetuates negative stereotypes about black people to the kind of racist white people who fuxwit black music but not so much black people, e.g. the University of Oklahoma chapter of Sigma Alpha Epsilon, which would never allow Wacka Flocka to join, despite their love for his music.

"Shake It Off" debuted at number one on the Hot 100. It was the 22nd song to do so and Taylor Swift's second number one song in the US. "Anaconda" peaked at number two, behind "Shake It Off." Nicki Minaj has yet to top the Billboard Hot 100.

"Shake It Off" stayed at number one for two weeks before it was supplanted by "All About That Bass," by Meghan Trainor, a song in which a disgusting fat (white) woman sings about how big her ass is, which remained number one for eight weeks straight.

Everything about Azealia Banks is also-ran status, including her name. Azealia Banks sounds like the name of a knockoff version of Iggy Azalea that your mom would buy you for your 13th birthday because it was $2 cheaper than the real thing, if a compact disc were still an appropriate gift for a child's 13th birthday.

There's speculation that, in fact, Iggy Azalea stole her name from Azealia Banks, but it's hard to say. They're both more or less the same age, and their careers both began to take off right around the same time, in 2K11. It wouldn't have made sense for Iggy Azalea to steal her name from Azealia Banks before anyone knew who Azealia Banks was because (a) how would she have known who Azealia Banks was? and (b) what good would it have done her, I mean if no one knew who Azealia Banks was? I'm pretty sure Azealia Banks is the source of this rumor. She's obsessed with the idea of Iggy Azalea stealing from black people. It's as much a part of who she is, at this point, as any other aspect of her career.

Iggy Azalea and Azealia Banks first got into it back when Iggy Azalea was chosen for the 2K12 Freshman 10 issue of XXL and Azealia Banks wasn't— this despite the fact that XXL doesn't usually include any women in its annual freshman class, and there was already a white person in this group, Mack-lemore. XXL was willing to bend over backwards to include Iggy Azalea, it seemed, but they didn't want shit to do with Azealia Banks.

Banks' "212," in fact, had been a viral sensation in 2K11 and bigger than anything Iggy Azalea had done up until that point, but she'd already begun to fade by the time the 2K12 Freshman 10 issue of XXL arrived six or eight months later. Whatever she followed "212" up with wasn't nearly as popular. I took a look at a few Azealia Banks videos once, after she succeeded—via trolling—to convince some people that her album Broke with Expensive Taste is some sort of artistic masterpiece, and that it's being suppressed because she's black, and honestly, they seemed a lot more creative to me than Iggy Azalea's videos, if not anything I'd actually want to watch. It seems like her music and her general aesthetic would appeal to gay guys, and in fact she was once briefly popular amongst fruits, but she's since torn her drawers with them, so to speak, by calling people the other f-word and accusing gay white guys of ripping off a lot of their slang from black women. Which is true. Gay white guys on sites like Gawker have built a cottage industry based on monitoring black women's Twitter accounts for content.

When Azealia Banks took to Twitter to complain that she'd been passed over for the cover of XXL in favor of Iggy Azalea, she seized upon the fact that Azalea once referred to herself as a runaway slave master. There's a line on one of her mixtapes that goes, "I'm a runaway slave... master." Try as I might, I'm at a loss for how this could be anything other than Iggy Azalea actually referring to herself as a slave master. The most I can think is that maybe she's saying that she's running away from being a slave master; like, she's seen the error of her ways and she's no longer pursuing that as a career. She issued an apology, which is something I never ever recommend, no matter how wrong you were, probably thinking that would satisfy Azealia Banks. It goes to show how furrin she really is. Azealia Banks continued to troll Iggy Azalea.

When the Eric Garner verdict was announced, in early December 2K14, Azealia Banks criticized Iggy Azalea for not having anything to say about it. "It's funny to see people like Igloo Australia silent when these things happen," she wrote. "Black culture is cool, but black issues sure aren't, huh?" Iggy Azalea hadn't been on Twitter that afternoon, but it's likely she wouldn't have had anything to say about the Eric Garner verdict if she had. By the time the Eric Garner verdict was announced there'd already been the initial video of Eric Garner getting choked out by 5-o, the Mike Brown shooting and the Mike Brown verdict, not to mention any number of other police shootings of unarmed black men that didn't become quite as famous. I don't recall Iggy Azalea having much, if anything, to say about any of those. It's not inconceivable that Iggy Azalea would have purposely avoided going on Twitter until that situation died down some.

In the interest of fairness, I should point out that a lot of black artists didn't have shit to say about the Black Lives Matter movement. The TIs must have told them they weren't allowed to. A few weeks later, on New Year's Eve, Kanye West dropped what was supposed to be the first single from his next album, which had already been pushed back from a prospective fall 2K14 release date, some garbage with Paul McCartney that's already long since been forgotten. In an interview to promote it, he explained that his father, supposedly a former Black Panther, told him he shouldn't address the Black Lives

Matter movement. He'd already pissed off white people enough with Yeezus, his father may have felt.

Azealia Banks recorded Broke with Expensive Taste while she was signed to Interscope, but the label decided it would rather not release the album, because she's batshit and no one seems to give a shit about her music, and it was decided she could retain the rights to the album, probably because it was advantageous to them for tax purposes. She released the album on a random Friday in November, as a surprise, to a resounding chorus of crickets. A year before, Beyoncé surprise-released an album on a random Friday and damn near broke the Internets. It's probably because she's more light-skinted.

In mid-December, Azealia Banks went up to Hot 97 to promote the album and also to air out Iggy Azalea and her black public cosigner T.I., who often jumps to her defense. This was just a YouTube video, not anything that was going on the air, so she was free to curse, break down in tears at multiple points during the course of the 45 min or so-long conversation and say things that might have caused her to get let go from a major label if she hadn't already. It's one of the more fascinating YouTube videos you'll see that doesn't have anything to do with 9/11 and certainly the most intentionally interesting thing Hot 97's been involved with in some time. Azealia Banks was having what's known amongst people who work with emotionally disturbed children as "an episode." In the most widely-excerpted bit, she wept as she complained about black music being "smudged out" by the Iggy Azaleas of the world.

Someone claiming to be Anonymous, clearly deeply affected by the Hot 97 video, threatened to release an Iggy Azalea sex tape if she didn't apologize to black people for cultural appropriation and not being sufficiently upset about the Eric Garner verdict. Rumors of an Iggy Azalea sex tape have been circulating for years. It's possible that there is an Iggy Azalea sex floating around the darkest, seediest corners of the Internets, and we just haven't heard about it.

When The Fappening took place, in the late summer of 2K14, supposedly some of those pics had been circulating for years, primarily on a message board called AnonIB. A few kids there figured out how to access pics that have been uploaded to the Apple cloud. When you take a picture with an iPhone, a copy of that picture is uploaded to Apple's own cloud storage, and god knows where else, and apparently their security is not very good. I wonder if someone figured out a flaw in the actual software or if they just called up claiming to be Jennifer Lawrence and said they forgot their password. Many high profile hacks, including Sarah Palin in the '08 presidential election, are just a matter of either guessing someone's password or figuring out the answers to those security questions for when you've lost your password, e.g. which elementary school you went to. Some of that shit you can just find in the wiki.

Supposedly, a guy Iggy Azalea used to date has a video of the two of them doing the nasty and he shopped it around to pron companies, but they can't do anything with it unless she signs off on it, and by the time she was famous enough for there to be any interest in an Iggy Azalea sex tape she was already making enough money from music that she didn't need a pron film on the market. Kim Kardashian was rich from the moment she was born, let alone by the time she dropped Kim K Superstar, but it's not like she can sing or dance or act or anything. Pron is the only thing she actually does, unless you count that iPhone game, from which I've heard she makes boatloads of money, possibly into the hundreds of millions. While those celebrity sex tapes released by pron companies are presented as if they've been stolen from a celeb's house or submitted by an angry ex Is Anyone Up-style, in fact both the guy and the girl have to sign off on its release, or else the pron company could probably be sued into Bolivian.

Azalea claims that the girl depicted in this sex tape isn't her, and also that she wasn't an adult when it was filmed… which makes me wonder if she actually viewed the sex tape as part of the process of deciding whether or not it should be released. Word on the street is that her ass in this sex tape doesn't look anything like it does now, but that could just be because her ass now is fake. She might suffer from body dysmorphia. When she says that the girl in the sex tape isn't her, it could just mean that her mind doesn't recognize the girl in the sex tape as being her because her ass doesn't look right. She was either 20 or 21 when her career began to take off in 2K11 and she's been an adult, for pron purposes, since 2008. If there's no way of determining exactly when it was filmed, it might not be legal to release anyway, regardless of whether or not Azalea is willing to participate. In the Arruh sex tape, for example, an episode of TRL was playing in the background. I think a Backstreet Boys video came on. So inappropriate.

Before the deadline by which Iggy Azalea was supposed to have apologized to the black community arrived, this Twitter account claiming to be Anonymous announced that it wouldn't actually release the Iggy Azalea sex tape, because that would be against their principles; they'd just release certain screencaps with her face in them but not any nudity or insertion, to prove that it's her and that they could release the entire thing if they wanted to, if she gets out of line again. She never did apologize to the black community, which might the most tragic thing in all of this (with all due respect to Eric Garner), if only because of how amusing that would have been. And "Anonymous" never did follow through with those screencaps, let alone the sex tape. The account they were using was deleted by Twitter not long after they announced that they were above leaking someone's sex tape. I'm thinking the TIs may have gotten in contact with someone at Twitter and maybe also someone in law enforcement, to the extent that the two aren't one in the same.

11.
Be Your Own Boss

*"I don't care how big the corporation backing you is.
If it's not your money, you're not the boss."*

— Dame Dash

You can get a sense of what it may have been like to work with Dame Dash back in the late '90s-early '00s from a scene in the movie Backstage.

Dame is backstage getting his hair cut and barking on then-Def Jam exec Kevin Liles over a disagreement about some jackets. Because Dame never seems to have had any hair to begin with, the barber is just kinda circling his head with a comb and a pair of clippers. Dame was agitated to the point where, if it had been necessary to use those clippers on his head, they may have exploded, like in the song "Can't Stop the Prophet" by Jeru the Damaja.

People who are proud of their success in business like getting haircuts because it gives them an opportunity to pontificate about how and why they've been so successful and what you can do to emulate their success. I'm sure part of the reason my play cousin Killer Mike owns a barber shop is because he's constantly bloviating, even when he's not on cable news.

Also, including a haircut scene in the film gave Dame the opportunity to show off the fact that he gets his haircut several times a week, if not on a daily basis. Suge Knight, who didn't have any hair either, made a similar boast in an article in either the Times Magazine or The Source back in the mid '90s—possibly both. Who can remember some shit that happened 20 years ago? You'd have to be young to have not killed enough brain cells yet; and if you're that young, you weren't around back then anyway.

If you can remember 1995, it's because you weren't there.

Dame was upset because Kevin Liles had given everyone on the tour Def

Jam jackets, not unlike something LL Cool J, the Beastie Boys and Public Enemy would have worn back in the mid to late '80s, when rap groups as disparate as NWA, MC Hammer and Salt N Pepa would go out on huge package tours. KRS-One and MC Shan would be on the same bill. Rap music wasn't big enough to sustain every garbage rapper bringing out his own weed carriers as opening acts, supplemented by local artists no one ever heard of... white juggalo kids who paid to get on the bill.

The jackets said Def Jam, which might have given someone the idea—if they saw, say, Ja Rule wearing one, on his way back to the hotel (via N2Deep) to make sweet, passionate love to several hoo-ers—that the tour had been booked by Def Jam rather than Roc-A-Fella. They'd be much more concerned about the jackets than the hoo-ers, in Dame's addled mind. Indeed, to hear Dame tell it, this jacket incident was part of a much larger pattern of behavior, in which Def Jam would purposely try to take credit for Roc-A-Fella Records initiatives. If Dame didn't check this shit right then and there, in front of the cameras, for inclusion in a forthcoming concert film, they might have tried to take credit for the Rocbox.

In interviews umpteen years after the fact, Kevin Liles is quick to point out the fact that he had to sign off on it in order for Dame to use that scene in the film. In mainstream films, like in pr0n, you can't just use someone's likeness without getting them to sign a release form—though in mainstream films it's not necessary to keep photocopies of documents proving that everyone who appeared in the film was at least 18 years of age on file with some shady Hispanic lawyer, possibly the same lady who was defending Adnan Syed, of Serial fame. It is necessary to include a disclaimer towards the end of the credits reel stating that you didn't harm any animals featured in the film, unless you really did harm and/or kill a few animals, like in HBO's Luck.

If Kevin Liles hadn't signed off on that scene of himself being so thoroughly ridiculed, and Dame used it anyway, Liles could have sued Dame for any money he made from Backstage, if Dame made any money from Backstage—and possibly even more than that, as a punitive measure, for any pain and suffering Liles endured as a result of such humiliation. There's no way a judge wouldn't have believed he was humiliated. Kevin Liles could have fucked around and owned that film. It would have been Kevin Liles Presents Backstage: Behind the Scenes of the Hard Knock Life Tour as Booked by Def Jam. Imagine how upset Dame would have been then.

Kevin Liles knew better than to do anything that might have led to further disagreement in the Def Jam building or caused Dame to have that guy Ty Ty pepper spray him. If only he'd had the sense to not sign off on that scene and then sue if Dame included it in the film.

Because he's so willing to tolerate abuse, and because he lacks either the sense or the balls to try to strike out on his own, Kevin Liles will always have a job with Lyor Cohen. He bolted Def Jam for the Warner Music Group when Lyor became the chairman there, in the mid '00s, which is what opened up the Def Jam presidency for Jay Z, and now he's working with Lyor on 300 Entertainment, Cohen's Illuminati-backed post-360 deal record label. I think he was even working for Lyor in some capacity in the period in between when Cohen left Warner Music Group and when he launched 300, when he was officially unemployed, just fixing him breakfast in the morning, running various errands, tucking him in at night and what have you.

It wasn't long after Backstage was released, in the early '00s, when Lyor first attempted to drive a wedge between Dame and Jay Z. He may have seen the film and decided that Dame had to go. He couldn't have Dame talking to Kevin Liles just any old way, knowing good and well Kevin Liles couldn't defend himself.

If Dame ever talked to Lyor like that, it wasn't included in the film. But I suspect that he didn't, because it wouldn't have ended as well for Dame if he did. Lyor, as discussed elsewhere in this book, is at least as big as Aesop Rock, and he's not constantly walking around in some SSRI-induced haze. If anything, he probably needs to be on some sort of prescription meds. He only lived in Israel briefly, but it may have been long enough to learn the same kind of karate that killed Roc Raida. And even if he didn't break a foot off in Dame's ass, he could have forwarded the matter to the Illuminati. It could have been arranged for Dame to be on that plane with Aliyah, his alleged fiancée.

Lyor is alleged to have approached Jay Z about selling his, Dame and Kareem "Biggs" Burke's remaining shares in Roc-A-Fella Records to Def Jam. The Roc-A-Fella-Def Jam joint venture had always been structured so that Def Jam would eventually purchase the remaining shares in the Roc, the amount they would pay to be determined by how many records Roc-A-Fella artists sold during their tenure with Def Jam. Hence, presumably, that period in the years leading up to the final dissolution of the old Roc-A-Fella, circa '04, when it seemed like literally anyone and everyone associated with the Roc could get a release date. We might have the structure of this deal to thank for Kanye's career. If only there was a way someone could go back in time and rewrite those contracts!

Def Jam would have eventually owned Roc-A-Fella Records outright anyway; this was just a matter of pushing the date of the sale up some for the purpose of getting rid of Dame. Def Jam, once the deal was done, would be able to do whatever they wanted to do with Roc-A-Fella, and of course they would have promptly dropped Dame and Biggs like a bad habit and installed Jay Z as the sole nominal figurehead of the Roc, working under the aforementioned Kevin Liles, probably with a hefty salary—his reward for kicking Dame to the curb.

This was still a few years before the time when a white man could approach Jay Z with a business deal that involved undermining another black man's interests and expect him to go through with it, so there was no Roc-A-Fella sale, at least not then.

It's been reported that, while he may have liked the idea of severing ties with Dame, with whom he didn't work closely in the years after his career blew up, Jay felt that such a deal would be disloyal. Dame spent years trying to get Jay a record deal, back when the Lyor Cohens of the world didn't want shit to do with Jay Z. Eventually, they started their own label to release Reasonable Doubt, probably funded by Biggs' drug money. The success of the terrible "Ain't No Dreaded N-Word," from Reasonable Doubt, probably due to Foxy Brown's appearance more so than Jay himself, led to both the joint venture with Def Jam and Foxy Brown's own deal with Def Jam. It should be pointed out, for the sake of hip-hop journalism, that Foxy Brown's Ill Na Na, with rhymes written by Jay Z, sold better than any Jay Z album had up to that point, though maybe just because she looked like chocolate-dipped sex on a stick, while Jay Z looked like Joe Camel.

A year later, Jay went on vacation somewhere over in the Mediterranean.

It was his first real vacation since his career blew up, and it was the beginning of chancletas-era Jay Z, kicking it on a boat with Beyoncé, showing off his middle-age man physique. Dame took this as an opportunity to fire several people from Roc-A-Fella, including a girl whose job was to bring Jay Z scarves and water, for when his brow was sweaty and his throat was parched, and install Cam'ron and Beanie Sigel, of all people, as co-vice presidents.

There's an entire segment of MTV's Diary of Jay Z on the fact that Beanie Sigel didn't even have what it takes to maintain a career as a rapper, a job for which there are no qualifications—you don't even have to know how to rap! Jay Z could hardly take Beanie Sigel to a night club without him threatening to kick someone's ass, and now he'd been made co-vice president.

Cam'ron is clearly insane. He suffers from IBS, which, I once heard on NPR, is psychological in nature and often caused by some childhood trauma, possibly something sexual. Sexual doesn't necessarily mean gay, but I don't know that there's anything straight that's sufficiently traumatizing as to cause irritable bowel syndrome in your 30s. There was never a time in my life when it was inappropriate for a woman to touch my junk. Ask the lady who gave me a CAT scan back in '96.

Meanwhile Lyor, who'd torn his drawers with the Universal Music Group, so to speak, over that time Feds ran up in the Def Jam building looking for evidence that Murder Inc was secretly financed by Kenneth "Supreme" McGriff, finagled a deal in which he'd become chairman of the Warner Music Group. He did so by telling the TIs who owned WMG that he could sign Jay Z, whose deal with Def Jam was coming to an end later that year. If WMG had been able to acquire Jay Z's services, who knows how much they would have made. Think about how much Jay Z's net worth has grown since the early to mid '00s, and think of how much the people who sign his checks must have made. Lyor Cohen rode that speculation straight to the bank.

Jay, Dame and Biggs, per the initial terms of their joint venture, sold their remaining shares in Roc-A-Fella Records to Def Jam for $10 million, of which they each received about $3 million. Jay Z, at that point, became a free agent and began exploring his options, including signing with Lyor at WMG. Dame wanted to continue to draw a salary from Def Jam to run Roc-A-Fella Records and berate people in the Def Jam building as if he had any real say in the matter. In interviews at the time, he spoke of Roc-A-Fella Records as if he'd continue to run it, with or without Jay Z, forever. Biggs, like a guy with one of those stimulus checks George W. Bush gave out to fix the economy (right around that same time, as I recall), probably bought a shedload of drugs in an attempt to double his $3 million and thus be able to buy every pair of Air Jordans there ever was.

Jay Z ended up playing Lyor against LA Reid, who'd replaced Lyor at Island Def Jam, to secure a deal with IDJ in which he received, among other things, the Def Jam presidency, which had recently been vacated by Kevin Liles, who doesn't fuxwit LA Reid, and the rights to his master recordings. The way those '90s deals worked, Jay would have eventually been able to re-record all of his Def Jam stuff, except maybe "Always Be My Sunshine," and upload it to online music stores himself anyway. It's the reason why Spotify is lousy with things like, say, an ostensibly note-for-note remake of "O.P.P." by a 40 some-odd year-old Treach.

Essentially, Jay snaked Dame the same way Lyor had proposed only a few years prior. He studied the TIs' techniques and then emulated them. Eventually, he'd internalize them to the point where they were second nature—and that's when the big bucks started rolling in...

Since then, Dame and Jay's careers have followed a more or less opposite trajectory. Jay Z started with a shedload of money and ended up with a truly obscene amount of money. Dame started with a shedload of money and now owes the government and various other creditors a shedload of money.

Needless to say, both because this shit happened over 10 years ago and because Dame Dash, Dame was relieved of his position with the Roc. He was given his own vanity imprint under Def Jam, with whoever was dumb enough to side with Dame over Jay. Kanye West, the only really viable artist left at Roc-A-Fella at that point, who'd been both signed and championed by Dame, sided with Jay. The Dame Dash Music Group was over and done with in about a year.

At that point, Dame shifted his focus to Rocawear, which had always been his baby. Jay Z was rarely if ever seen in the Rocawear offices and never exhibited any real interest in fashion. When Dame and Jay were on the outs, after Dame tried to destroy the Roc by putting Cam'ron and Beanie Sigel in charge, Dame shifted his base of operations to the Rocawear offices, to avoid Jay Z.

Perhaps in an attempt to spite Jay Z, because of what went down with Def Jam and Roc-A-Fella, Dame began trying to bleed Rocawear of as much cash as he could possibly wring from it. He had Rocawear paying the rent on an expensive-ass apartment in London, England, and he was trying to get Rocawear to cut seven-figure checks to people from that Kevin Bacon movie he produced to pose for ads. It was only at that point that Jay Z took an interest in Roc-A-Fella. The two Russian guys who'd been given a stake in the company, having been recommended by Russell Simmons, may have explained to Jay that they could sell Rocawear for boatloads of money, the same way Simmons sold Phat Farm, but not if Dame drove it out of business first.

The way the Rocawear deal was structured, if Jay ever sided with the Russian guys over Dame, they could essentially drive Dame out of the company. They may not have been able to force Dame to sell his shares, if he didn't want to, but they could put him in a position in which he had no say in how the company was run. There's no way Dame would have been able to accept a situation like that. He probably would have made way more money that way and wouldn't have a negative net worth in 2K15, but that's just not the way things are done in Harlem.

Dame sold his shares in Rocawear for $22 million, of which he received $7 million in cash. A few years later, Jay sold the company for $200 million.

———————

Joie "Joey IE" Manda worked under Lyor Cohen at Warner Music Group, where Lyor is said to have pioneered the 360 deal.

Invented to make up for the loss in revenue from illegal downloading, in a 360 deal, the label gets a percentage of any other money an artist might receive, including endorsements, touring, merch, reality shows and what have you, in addition to any money the artistic could theoretically receive from album sales. It's a way more ridonkulous, draconian version of the classic 20th century record deal, which was already considered one of the worst deals you could possibly sign.

At Atlantic Records, one of the labels under the WMG umbrella, Manda signed b- and c-list southern rappers like my old friend Bun B, Paul Wall, Wacka

Flocka and Rawse's weed carriers (but not Rawse himself) to 360 deals. These were not necessarily the kind of signings you'd brag about to anyone who knows from rap music, but WMG must have made a shedload of money from them, if Manda's subsequent career trajectory is any indication. It's hard to say, because he could be having so much success in his career because he's white. LOL

Meanwhile Lupe Fiasco, who'd been signed to Atlantic since before the Lyor era, complained that he couldn't get a release date once 360 deals became the norm. He claims he was told either he had to sign a new "slave" deal or they just wouldn't bother with him. He had to resort to stunts like threatening to retire from rap music and trying to get Lupe stans from the Internets to sleep in tents in the street outside Atlantic Records' offices.

In the late '00s, Dame released a couple of albums by stoner-rap journeyman Curren$y, from an art gallery run out of a building he was squatting in on the Lower East Side. Curren$y may never have been officially signed to Dame, which is not considered necessary in Harlem. Curren$y was embraced by the Hipster Music Mafia, in part due to lobbying on his behalf by Tom Breihan, then with Pitchfork, who makes Lyor Cohen look like Ian Cohen, and this may have led to a deal with Atlantic Records, if sheer talent alone wasn't enough for him to become labelmates with the rest of the clowns Joey IE signed there.

After Curren$y signed with Atlantic, Dame released a Curren$y album called Muscle Car Chronicles. Dame alleges that Joey IE then forced Curren$y to sue Dame Dash, ordering Muscle Car Chronicles pulled from shelves, because Curren$y, per his new "slave" deal, wasn't allowed to release albums on any other labels, and if he didn't sue Dame, WMG would sue Curren$y. Dame later claimed in an interview that he's sued WMG for tortious interference, for forcing Curren$y to sue him, explaining that, by trying to have Muscle Car Chronicles pulled from shelves, they were interfering with his ability to make money. Like a brother in the joint who has to work on his own case (no Boutros), Dame has become somewhat of an expert on the law. He's constantly in court, or due in court, because he owes money all over town, and he doesn't always bring a lawyer. He says lawyers charge money out the ass just to pay a paralegal $10/hour to do all the grunt work, so why not just hire a paralegal yourself and save millions of dollars. In fact, some of the people suing him are lawyers he never paid.

Dame regularly uses Instagram to go off on the people he sees as being responsible for his current financial situation, including Lyor Cohen, Joey IE and the lawyer who represents his babies' mothers in family court. He once posted a picture of Cohen, Russell Simmons, Jay, Dame and Biggs on the day the Def Jam-Roc-A-Fella joint venture was signed. Lyor was the only one smiling, and Dame said it was because Lyor was happy to be making money from someone else's culture, since he can't make any money from his own culture. Culture vulture is Dame Dash's pet name for people who seek to profit from someone else's culture because they can't make any money from their own culture.

Shortly thereafter, Dame posted a picture of Joey IE, whom he called "a culture vulture's dimwitted assistant," i.e. not even someone who's worthy of being considered a culture vulture himself, like Lyor Cohen, given his track record at Atlantic Records and later with Def Jam, where he replaced Jay Z as president, and Interscope, where he's the head of urban music. Dame accused Joey IE of using divide and conquer tactics on people who are actually from the culture, presumably referring to the Muscle Car Chronicles lawsuit. Some of Dame's Instagram captions must run into the hundreds of words, but it's never quite clear what he's talking about—and his interviews don't always help matters either.

Funkmaster Flex caught wind of Dame's Instagram post about Joey IE, and he couldn't have Dame going off on Joey IE any more than Lyor Cohen could have Dame going off on Kevin Liles. Joey IE began his career with Funkmaster Flex, bringing Flex scarves and water, for when his brow was sweaty and his throat was parched. In return, Joey IE was given a credit on at least one of those 60 Minutes of Funk mixtape albums Flex dropped back in the mid to late '90s. I once joked on the Internets that Flex let Joey IE have sex with his sister. Hopefully, people understood that was a joke. I'm not even sure if Flex has a sister; and it's not appropriate for a guy to give a girl to another guy as a gift or payment for a service rendered, unless the girl is cool with it, in which case it's morally okay (but it might still be illegal). Joey IE, by then, was in charge of black music at Interscope, and Funkmaster Flex was in the perfect position to benefit from his largesse, if not in return for anything IE did with Flex's sister, then because I'm sure Interscope has plenty of records Hot 97 listeners wouldn't otherwise be interested in hearing. Note that I'm not necessarily suggesting anything illegal. As was the case with Flex's family tree, we don't have enough facts to be able to say for certain.

Flex responded to Dame's Instagram post about Joey IE by spending just shy of half an hour on Hot 97 ranting and raving about Dame, recounting the history of Roc-A-Fella Records (not as well as I've done here), defending Joey IE and suggesting Dame stick to the art that was on display in the building he was squatting in. Dame had some white kids in there doing the actual painting, but he may have sold some of their work and pocketed the money. One of them might be the person behind a campaign on—where else?—Instagram called Dame Dash Owes Me Money.

Dame responded to Flex's rant on the radio with a post on Instagram in which he lamented the fact that Flex would "cape" for a culture vulture. He also offered to come up to Hot 97, where the two of them could work out their differences live on air, and he could explain why he feels that Lyor Cohen and Joey IE are culture vultures. Flex has yet to take Dame up on this offer, per-haps realizing that he could use Dame to driving ratings without having Dame there in the building, which might lead to more problems with the landlord, and that anything Dame said about Joey IE could interfere with any consider-ation Flex might receive from Interscope.

What Dame needed was someone who was interested in using asinine beef to drive ratings, who was far enough outside the industry that he didn't have to sweat any potential reaction from Interscope.

Dame and Combat Jack go way back, Combat having managed Dame when the latter first began his career in artist management, in his late teens. Dame had a couple of groups, one of which featured Ski Beatz, who produced on Reasonable Doubt and Camp Lo's brilliant Uptown Saturday Night, and both of which landed deals with major labels. Combat helped Dame negotiate these deals, and as a result the then-teenager is said to have pocketed upwards of a hundred grand.

Of course that hundred grand, or whatever it was, didn't last any longer than the money Dame received from being extricated from Jay Z's business af-fairs, and eventually Dame was having to borrow money from Combat to take a cab back and forth to Combat's offices. Dame didn't want to take the train, because people from Harlem can't be seen riding the train, and in fact it isn't even clear why the train stops in Harlem (if it does—I'm from Missouri).

Combat then helped Dame shop Jay Z to major labels. When they couldn't find any takers, because major labels are run by culture vultures who don't know from rap music, Jay and Dame started Roc-A-Fella Records with an investment from Kareem "Biggs" Burke, perfectly legit businessman, some of which they used to fly down to somewhere in the Caribbean, where they shot the video for "In My Lifetime," and to rent that yacht. The villa was borrowed from one of Biggs' associates in whatever line of work he was in at the time. Combat helped Jay, Dame and Biggs land a single deal with the label that put out "In My Lifetime" and an album deal with the label that put out Reasonable Doubt. He's intimated to randos on Twitter that these weren't the most lucrative deals in the world.

Alas, they were amongst the last deals Combat did with Dame, Jay et al. Two decades after the fact, Dame says that Combat tried to "fleece" Roc-A-Fella, and that's why Dame stopped working with him. He says the Roc was trying to negotiate a deal in which they'd get paid based on the gross rather than the net, but Combat tried to get them to sign a contract that said the exact opposite; Jay Z caught it just in time, or else they would have been screwed. It may have just been a matter of the Roc-A-Fella co-founders, like every other rapper there ever was, and like any black man whose freedom is on the line, if he has any sense, preferring a Jewish lawyer, and this may have led to Combat's current obsession with white privilege, which he spends at least 20 minutes of each episode of The Combat Jack Show discussing.

This was the second time Dame had been on The Combat Jack Show. The first time was one of the best episodes of The Combat Jack Show of all time, of ALL TIME, right up there with the two Touré episodes. Dame spent much of the episode antagonizing Just Blaze, whom Dame and Jay bullied when he was a house producer for the Roc, along with Kanye West. There's a scene in the movie Fade to Black (not to be confused with the superior Backstage) in which Jay clowns Just Blaze for spending the time he should have been spending working on beats for the Black Album trying to buy old video games. In that first Dame episode, we learned that Just Blaze took too long working on the beat for that song "Champions" from the Paid in Full soundtrack, so Dame gave it to Kanye, who turned it around in a single afternoon. There's also plenty of talk of Just Blaze's many sartorial mishaps, including the time he bought a bandulu New York Jets jersey and the time he received a rhinestone belt in the mail while he was working in the studio. Just Blaze's response to this abuse, then and now, was along the lines of Kevin Liles response in Backstage—or lack thereof.

The Return of Dame Dash episode was hot garbage. We didn't learn any more about Dame's beefs with Lyor and Joey IE than we did from reading the captions of the pics he posted on Instagram. Combat was at a loss for how to control Dame or guide the flow of the conversation, which would have been fine if Dame had someone there to publicly humiliate, but Just Blaze has long since found better things to do than sit there in the studio with Combat and god knows who else and recuse himself from any discussions of the music biz to which he may have been able to contribute.

Eventually, Dame began interviewing Combat, asking Combat to put a culture vulture on notice, since Dame himself had spent the entire episode up to that point not quite explaining his beefs with Lyor and Joey IE. You could hear the wheels turning in Combat's head for entirely too long, for someone who knows the music biz inside and out, before he finally settled on Steve Stoute. Combat Jack has a Steve Stoute story that he shares on every third episode of The Combat Jack Show, in between the Bevel commercial and the white privilege discussion. I only repeat it here for the benefit of people who have no idea who any of these people are.

Steve Stoute used to work with rappers like Kid 'n Play, Nas and Will Smith, and he was an exec with Interscope back in the pre-Joey IE era. Combat, back when he was still a lawyer, helped Foxy Brown's brother Gavin land a deal with Interscope. As part of the deal, Combat claims that Steve Stoute demanded a kickback from Gavin. Essentially, Gavin would have to slide Steve Stoute some of the money he received from Interscope or else the deal was off the table. Combat claims this was Steve Stoute's m.o. back then. When he heard that Stoute tried to pull this shit on Foxy Brown's brother, whose deal wasn't for much anyway, Combat says he called Steve Stoute and told him to waive the kickback or else Combat would call Interscope founder Jimmy Iovine and tell him Steve Stoute was out here charging artists a fee to sign to the label. Stoute reluctantly agreed to waive the fee.

Years later, Combat saw Steve Stoute walking down the street and tried to shake his hand. Stoute gave Combat a limp hand that Combat compared to a scarf, like the one Joey IE used to bring Funkmaster Flex. I consulted the wiki re: Steve Stoute, for another project I was working on, and it said that he has gout, a form of arthritis that comes from eating cheese and drinking beer. I checked again, for that article I wrote about Dame, and the part about him having gout had been removed, possibly because Stoute had been contacted by gout charities. I took a look at the wiki's edit function, and whoever had the part about gout removed had an email address from Stoute's company, Translation.

Most guests on episodes in which Combat shares his Steve Stoute story have their own Steve Stoute story, and Dame Dash was no exception. He says that Junior Mafia used to put makeup and a wig on Stoute while he slept, on tour. There's a famous video of Lil Cease from Junior Mafia giving a room full of people the "whirly bird" backstage at one of their shows, which makes me wonder if that's all they did to Steve Stoute. Dame also alleged that he slapped the shit out of Steve Stoute and kicked him out of his office for reneging on a bet.

There was also plenty of discussion of Dame's various philosophies on business. It didn't quite rise to the level of his legendary appearances on Sirius XM's Sway in the Morning and Power 105's The Breakfast Club, but it was more informative than what he had to say about Lyor and Joey IE, if not at all useful. Much of it was as wrong as it was ostensibly well-intentioned.

Dame Dash believes that you should never save money. He doesn't, and presumably that's one of the reasons his net worth has a minus sign and seven digits. Better to owe millions of dollars all over town and constantly be at risk of getting locked up for any number of financial reasons, including tax evasion and failure to pay child support, than to put your money in the bank and thus not be as motivated to make money as someone whose freedom depends on making millions of dollars, he might argue.

Arguably, he's sorta kinda got a point, but I don't know. I think I'd rather just have money in the bank and not be motivated to do anything with my life. I'm already halfway there. All I need is the money in the bank.

Dame is also very adamant about putting up your own money in any business you're involved with. He believes that you can never be the boss of a company you don't own, even if you've been given some position as nominal figurehead, like the one he hoped to maintain at a post-Jay Z Roc-A-Fella Records. If it's not your company, the TIs can always just snatch your job out from under you and give it to someone who actually has potential to make the company some money.

Again, this is at least kinda true. Dame's own life is proof that, as he likes to say, if it's not your company, you're not the boss.

Alas, that's no way to make money in 2K15. Dame's life is also proof that putting up your own money in every business venture you're involved with is an easy way to end up broke as an MFN joke when they don't succeed. Putting up as little of your own money as you possibly can, in a business venture in which you still get paid if the company does succeed, is just plain sound investment strategy. Mark Zuckerberg only owned some small percentage of Facebook stock, and I don't see him sweating it. Bono had some tiny fraction of what Zuckerberg had, and he's also a billionaire.

The one argument I can see for black people owning companies outright, and running said companies, is that it's the only way to get a business to hire a significant number of black people. Er, let me correct that: It's the only way to get a business where you don't have to wear a name tag to hire a significant number of black people. No offense to my white brothers and sisters, who hopefully actually paid for this book, but let's keep it real: White people aren't gonna do it. They've had 400 years, and the best they've been able to do is stop forcing people to work for free (officially).

We don't have another 400 years to wait for black people to start getting the kind of BS—and yet (relatively) high-paying—corporate jobs white chicks get, like the one where you talk on the phone with job applicants in an attempt to ascertain their race before you call them in for an actual interview. Cops are out here shooting black kids dead in the street as if they were dogs because the city can only raise but so much in tax revenue. The situation has become dire to the point where even Dame Dash's business ideas are starting to sound not half bad.

12.
Throw Your Hands In The Air

"When I grabbed him the only way I can describe it is I felt like a five-year-old holding onto Hulk Hogan."
— Darren Wilson

As far as Darren Wilson knew, Mike Brown and Dorian Johnson hadn't done anything other than walk in the middle of the street rather than on the side of the road or on the sidewalk, if there was a sidewalk.

Later, Wilson would claim that he heard a description of two suspects who'd been accused of stealing a box of cigarillos from Ferguson Market, and Mike Brown and Dorian Johnson fit that description, but the description he said he heard didn't match what actually went out over the dispatch. He must not have thought to find out what exactly it said before he said he heard it.

Admittedly, it can be off-putting to see people constantly walking up and down the street in a residential area, if you've never lived in an economically depressed area. It's one of the things I've had to adjust to, living in my house in a shanty town. At any hour of the day or night, you can look out the window and see someone walking down the street. I suspect that at least some of them are on their way to buy drugs. I could care less if they buy and use drugs, but I don't need them looking at my car or house and getting any bright ideas.

Johnson, in an interview he gave to local TV news shortly after Mike Brown was shot and killed, claims that Officer Wilson shouted an expletive at them and told them to get on the sidewalk. To his credit, Wilson wasn't accused of using the dreaded n-word. He was at least somewhat respectful. Of course he denies shouting an expletive at Mike Brown and Dorian Johnson.

Johnson told the local TV news that he told Wilson that they were already near where they were headed, and therefore it wasn't necessary for them to get on the sidewalk.

In retrospect, they might have considered just getting on the sidewalk. They were on their way to Johnson's house to smoke weed, at like 10:00 in the morning, which is why they needed those cigarillos. There was no need to have their stash on them when they went to the store, unless Johnson was living with seven or eight ne'er-do-well relatives and he didn't trust leaving it in the house, a distinct possibility in an area like Ferguson, but let's face it. These weren't the sharpest pencils in the box. No disrespect to the dead.

Dorian Johnson's account of what happened next, as delivered on local TV news that afternoon, struck me as suspect from jump. He came off like the guy in a Chinese restaurant—known in the STL as a Chinaman—who tries to argue that last time he only got four crab rangoon and therefore this time he should get six, as if the Chinese can't do math. It wasn't necessarily anything he said; it was just a vibe he gave off, though obviously there was the matter of the weed. He didn't want to explain to the local TV news that they were on their way to his house to smoke a blunt for breakfast, as if it wouldn't have come out in the investigation—a potential employer could have been watching!

I can't tell you that I wouldn't have done the same thing. America doesn't need to know every single thing that I do.

Johnson claims that Darren Wilson grabbed Mike Brown and tried to pull him into his car. Wilson of course claims that Brown reached into the car and tried to grab his gun. Mike Brown's DNA was found inside the car and on the gun, which Wilson was allowed to bring back to the station and personally enter into evidence—a clear violation of protocol in cases where a cop shoots someone dead in the street, though that may have just been a matter of the Ferguson Police Department not knowing what to do in that situation. It's not every day they kill someone, and in fact, normally there aren't very many murders in that area. It's not the awful ghetto you might expect.

The gun went off inside the car and struck Mike Brown in his hand. At that point, Mike Brown and Dorian Johnson took off running. Darren Wilson gave chase, eventually catching up with Mike Brown, the larger of the two suspects and the one who'd just been shot in the hand. When you're running from a bear in the woods and there's another guy there with you, your best bet is to shoot the other guy, especially if he's faster than you. You could shoot the bear, but if all you've got is a handgun, that's not nearly enough to stop the bear. That's just gonna piss him off. Even a rifle won't necessarily stop him, if you don't hit him in just the right place.

Cops in areas like Ferguson are like bears, in a sense, except with a bear at least you can try to play dead and maybe they won't bother you. Bears don't like to eat things that are already dead. They like to kill something and eat it right there on the spot, in part because bears are assholes, hence Yogi Bear stealing people's picnic baskets, and in part because if something's already dead it might not be fresh. The riots that erupted in Ferguson the night the Mike Brown verdict was announced are like the forest fires Yogi Bear is always trying to prevent. If only they'd reached the police station. But let's not get too far ahead of ourselves.

Mike Brown was still a good distance away from Darren Wilson when Wilson caught up with him, but it was only a matter of time before Wilson got close enough to throw cuffs on him. I saw a reconstruction of the crime scene put together by some young guy on Twitter. There was no good journalism that came out of the Mike Brown shooting, but some of the best of what there was came from random people on Twitter. At that point, Wilson says that Mike Brown turned toward him and started charging at him, and therefore he was left with no choice but to shoot Brown six more times. According to the autopsy, it was the last of those shots, to the head, that was fatal. Brown most likely would have survived the rest of them.

Accounts differ as to how necessary it was for Wilson to shoot Mike Brown so many times. Wilson of course says he had no choice in the matter. Witnesses and also Dorian Johnson, in that interview that didn't sit quite right with me, say that Mike Brown had his hands up and that he told Wilson that he didn't have a gun. I could almost see wanting to attack someone who only shot you once, in the hand; that's one of the worst places you can get shot, and someone who would do that is inconsiderate, to say the least. But I can't imagine that Mike Brown posed much of a threat to Darren Wilson after he'd been shot three or four times. The purpose of those last few shots may have been to finish him off, lest he survive and start issuing statements about what really happened in that car.

––––––––––––

A crowd began to gather near where Mike Brown lay dead in the street. His body lay there for a good four hours before someone finally came along and rolled him into the back of an SUV that probably took him to a morgue. For a while there, they didn't even bother to cover him. His mom showed up, and she could see him lying dead in the street like some grotesque museum exhibit. Again, this may have been a matter of Ferguson PD not being sure what to do. The most they could think was to give him a ticket for Illegal Lying Dead in the Street, and that wouldn't have looked right with all of those people there, many of whom I'm sure had warrants.

Pictures of Mike Brown's body lying dead in the street and stories about how the cops had shot him for no apparent reason spread like wildfire on Black People Twitter. Sometimes I stop by my parents' house on a Sunday afternoon after work to have a few free beers and pick up any mail I may have received. It's between where I work and my house in a shanty town. I don't work there nearly as often as I used to, because management is trying to force me to quit by working me as little as they can without firing me, at which point I could apply for unemployment, but I'll stop by anyway, for the free beer. I was sitting there having a beer that Sunday, when I first heard about the Mike Brown shooting.

Cops with military equipment showed up long before Mike Brown's ride got there, which makes me wonder how close they were, and why. A couple of years before the Mike Brown shooting, people began noticing tanks riding up and down the street in certain parts of St. Louis. Local TV news caught up with someone from the Army, who said they were just there conducting training exercises, not to blow random people in the hood to smithereens.

In the 1950s, the Army sprayed some sort of dust that gives you cancer from the tops of buildings in the part of St. Louis where most of my family lived at the time, where my old man grew up, as part of an experiment. They said that part of St. Louis closely resembled certain cities in Russia. Some people in my family later did come down with cancer, but the thing is, so many people get cancer these days. I've heard estimates that one in every two people will get cancer at some point in our lifetime. Something to look forward to!

When I first saw pics on Twitter of tanks in downtown St. Louis on their way to Ferguson, in the days following the Mike Brown shooting, there was no pretense of this being a training exercise. They weren't there to practice shooting Iraqis, they were there to actually shoot Americans. That's what they were practicing a few years ago. Again, Alex Jones somehow managed to predict the future.

People feared the Ferguson Police Department long before they were armed to the teeth with equipment they probably had no idea how to use, but not because they might launch a grenade up your ass. If they killed you, they wouldn't have any way to charge you money out the ass for ridonkulous speeding tickets. They could give you a ticket for Illegal Lying Dead in the Street, but how would you pay it?

A few days after the Mike Brown shooting, I wrote an article that broke down everything that happened in Ferguson, and the problems in that area that led to something like this eventually happening. I had everything that was in the Department of Justice report, and I had it a good seven months before it came out. There wasn't a single reporter that nailed the story like I did, not because I'm such a great writer—my primary focus is on talking shit about rappers on the Internets—but because no one really gave a shit. Mainstream media outlets sent down their token black guys, from the mailroom, or someone who didn't know what they were doing, who was looking to make a name for himself. They were less concerned with getting the actual story than with getting someone to argue with Don Lemon about who threw something first, the protesters or the police, which admittedly, was the second-best journalism to come out of Ferguson.

As explained in the Department of Justice report, the Ferguson Police Department, as well as the police in neighboring municipalities, of which there are so many, prey on people who drive through there. Most of the budgets for the city governments in those areas come from traffic fines and what have you. They pull over anyone who comes through driving so much as a mile over the speed limit, and if they can't find anyone speeding—because people who live there know better than to exceed the speed limit—they just pull someone over and claim they weren't driving exactly between the lines, or some such bullshit. They've got it set up so that seemingly every little town in that area has

a piece of the roads and highways that lead to the airport, including Natural
Bridge and the Inner Belt. In a one-mile stretch of the highway, you might
drive through five different towns.

If the Department of Justice was really concerned with justice, they would
have busted that shit up a long time ago. As it is, they haven't actually done
anything in Ferguson. They've identified the problem, but they've yet to
eliminate it.

All told, St. Louis County has upwards of 100 local municipalities. Some
of them are decent-sized cities unto themselves, while others only consist of a
handful of houses. They probably couldn't raise enough in tax revenue to fund
a police department, and whatever else a town with 79 people in it needs to
function. Hence the ridonkulous, draconian traffic-law enforcement. Many of
the smaller municipalities used to just be unincorporated St. Louis County,
but the State of Missouri forced them to incorporate in order to pass bullshit
laws designed to keep black people from buying houses there, back when it
was all white. Eventually, a few black people managed to buy houses there
anyway (these aren't the best houses in the world), causing most of the white
population to hightail it to areas south and west of there, like where Darren
Wilson lived. Now you've got mostly black people living in these towns that
wouldn't be towns in the first place if they hadn't once been "sundown towns."

The city where I went to college, Chicken Switch, MO, was once a sundown town. There was a big billboard out at the edge of town that read,
"Dreaded n-word, don't let the sun go down on your back in Chicken Switch."
Now it just says, "Welcome to Chicken Switch, MO, home of Josephine Baker
State University." They had to put up a sign announcing you'd (truly) arrived
because the city itself is hardly distinguishable from the hundreds of miles of
corn fields surrounding it in each direction. You could easily drive right past it
and end up in Iowa somewhere.

A guy I know once lived in a house across the street from a police station
in one of those towns. The police station was in what otherwise looked like
regular-ass house, but with a sign out front that said police station. I wonder
where they put people, if they have to lock people up. Do they just lock
you in the basement, chained to a stack pipe, like the gimp in Pulp Fiction?
They might have to drop you off at a St. Louis County facility. In addition

to each town's own local police, there's a St. Louis County police department, known as the County Brown. I think they just cover unincorporated areas, but don't start me to lying. I know they were involved in pointing guns at people for no apparent reason and firing tear gas canisters at people for standing around in the street, which as I recall from the 11th grade, is your right per one of the first few amendments of the Constitution, where it's referred to as "peaceable assembly."

So this police station was across the street from the guy's house, but actually it was in a different jurisdiction. He bought the house for a sandwich and a song—I'm talking Detroit prices here. The next day, he showed up to move his stuff in, and someone had stolen all of the copper pipes in the basement. He went across the street to the police station to report that his pipes had been stolen, and the cops were like, "Sorry, bro. That's not our jurisdiction." His police station was probably some other house half a mile down the road. Regardless of where the real police station is, I'd be concerned that someone managed to steal the plumbing from a house across the street from a police station. In fact, I'd wonder if the cops didn't take those pipes themselves. Cops in that area are notoriously corrupt.

Hearing this story, I couldn't help but be reminded of the episode of Sanford and Son where some guy told Lamont there were precious metals in his basement, and if he could go down there and extract them, they could share the proceeds. The guy went down there, removed all of the copper pipes and sold them for scrap, prompting Fred Sanford to call Lamont a big dummy. That show was as hilarious as it was informative.

Race riots usually start when angry black people, in the dog days of summer, witness the cops kill a black kid for no apparent reason, get upset and start setting fires, looting stores and throwing things at the police... and I'm thinking that's why the police showed up in such ridonkulous force almost immediately after Darren Wilson popped several caps in Mike Brown's ass. Calls went out not just to other Ferguson cops but also County Brown and any number of nearby municipalities, including some towns no one ever heard of. Whether or not the town that stole those pipes was involved I'm not sure. I don't know the name of that town.

At some point, there must have been damn near as many cops there as people. The cops, at least in some cases, had their guns drawn, and some of them came equipped with things they shouldn't even own in a town with 79 people in it. You wondered where they even kept that shit, in some of those police stations. The people were just standing around mourning the death of one of their neighbors and observing as the cops seemingly sabotaged the investigation. Did they really leave Mike Brown lying in the street because they wanted to gather as much evidence as they could before they moved him elsewhere, to make sure justice was served, or because they wanted to figure out the best way for Darren Wilson to cop a plea? Just because these people live in Ferguson doesn't mean that they're stupid.

It's likely that people wouldn't have rioted if there hadn't been such an overwhelming police presence, and if it wasn't so clear that justice wasn't about to be served. Anyway, it wasn't clear what purpose having so many heavily-armed cops there served once people actually started rioting. For the next few days, I watched local TV news reports showing people running from rim shops with gigantic car rims under their arms. Most people probably couldn't carry more than one of those things at a time, so groups of looters must have had to coordinate their efforts. I'm not sure what you can do with just one rim. Even people in the hood who put $5,000 worth of rims on a $1,000 car wouldn't ride around with just one rim. Besides, it would be too obvious. Everyone would know you came up on that one rim in the riots.

Some people were shown running up in Quik Trip, before it burned to the ground, running out with a bag of Funyuns or some shit. A few people came up on Skittles. If only there'd been time to disconnect the knockoff Slurpee machine and wheel it out of there before the place burned to the ground. Imagine how cool it would be to have that in your house. You could weez the juice whenever you felt like it. Nullus. I seem to recall Tommy Lee from Mötley Crüe having a Starbucks in his house on an episode of MTV Cribs back in the early 2000s. That's the white people equivalent of having a fake Slurpee machine in your house.

My thought with regard to stealing a bag of Funyuns from a Quik Trip during a race riot is that, if you're that desperate for a bag of potato chips, they should just let you have it. There shouldn't be an investigation to try to find out who stole those Funyuns. If the government made sure that people weren't so hungry that they'd risk life and limb, not to mention their freedom, to steal junk food during a riot, this wouldn't have been an issue. And the store—and everything in it—was gonna burn down anyway.

Later, the police did in fact make a big show of trying to bust people who looted that Quik Trip. They showed surveillance footage on the news and asked people to call in if they recognized any of the suspects. My little brother kinda looked like one of the kids running out of there with some Skittles. Hardly a week goes by when he doesn't resemble someone wanted by the police. He has a certain look. The police probably put more work into trying to find out who got some free shit from Quik Trip than they did in trying to find out what really happened in the Mike Brown shooting. Though I doubt anyone actually called that tip line.

The cops told the media they weren't allowed to cover the riots, and some of them actually complied. As far as I know, there wasn't a state of martial law declared, like in New Orleans after Hurricane Katrina, in which Blackwater mercenaries were allowed to shoot people dead on sight. It didn't make sense to me that reporters were allowed to cover the Iraq War from right there on the front lines but they were being told to return to their hotels in some bullshit suburb of St. Louis. I'm pretty sure the cops were just pulling rules out of their asses. Later, I read that the cops tried to randomly declare a curfew, and a court had to rule that they weren't allowed to do that.

Some of the best reporting to come out of Ferguson, for what it's worth, came from people livestreaming. There's some contraption you can connect to your iPhone that allows you to stream live video that hundreds of thousands or maybe even millions of people can watch via YouTube or various knockoff versions of YouTube. News organizations, including the mighty RT, would then go over someone's live stream for especially interesting bits that they could then license to show on air, thus raising the question of how come they couldn't just send their own guy there and have him livestream.

Twitter was either vital in organizing the nascent Black Lives Matter movement or a sad, cynical mess of people trolling and attention whoring, depending on how you look at it. Or maybe both, I guess. You had a lot of people out there doing the thing where you repost reports from mainstream media outlets as if you were there reporting live yourself. It's good for driving faves and retweets, which are good for driving your follower count. If you get enough followers, brands will pay you money to tweet ads. Some of the most popular Twitter accounts can get paid hundreds of thousands of dollars per tweet.

I'm sure some people honestly did have the best of intentions and the purest of motives, though it wasn't always clear to me what good they were doing. I guess at the very least they were helping get the word out, in case anyone hadn't heard. The level of discourse on Black People Twitter is such that I'm sure there's at least a few people who just got out of jail. Much of what self-styled, Twitter-based activists do involves taking information that already exists on the Internets and ratcheting up the emotional potency by isolating the most sensational bits of text and the most graphic images.

Meanwhile, all throughout the Mike Brown shooting and the subsequent protests you had people who could clearly give a rat's ass about the Black Lives Matter movement. It was weird to go on Twitter, say, the night the Darren Wilson verdict was announced and see cam hoo-ers—the true pioneers of livestreaming—advertising their shows, trying to get some poor bastard to give them a dollar to briefly show their vagines, and white rap fans joking about how some group named Migos is better than The Beatles, posting pics of things that supposedly exploded after hearing a Migos mixtape, while actual buildings were burning to the ground in Ferguson.

I'm not saying people shouldn't be allowed to discuss what they want to discuss on Twitter. I'm just saying. Nights like that, you find out where people stand.

———————————

I was at that Run the Jewels show the night the verdict was announced.

That afternoon, on their way to St. Louis, RTJ's tour bus got stuck on the highway in what looked like Illinois. They posted a picture of the broken down bus on Twitter, and I can tell the difference between random stretches of highway in Missouri and Illinois. The problem with the bus may have been a matter of Killer Mike trying to sit on the same side of the bus as El-P and Despot and damaging the suspension. At any rate, they had to be driven here in a panel van. A panel van is sometimes known—to insensitive people—as a rapist van, and in fact, there's a line on the second Run the Jewels album about a rapist van, which they refer to as a rape van, maybe because it's been a while since they were in high school. Later their merch trailer caught fire and weed carriers got stuck.

RTJ were scheduled to make an in-store appearance at a local record store called Vintage Vinyl. I figured there might be protests on that block. A week before, I was on that same street to see that Nas movie, Time Is Illmatic, and not long before I got there people had been doing that thing where they pretended to lie dead in the street. Sometime they did that on the actual highway, which fucked up rush hour traffic even more than it would have been otherwise—I guess all the better to get the point across.

Because I was going to a concert, and because I was anxious about the impending announcement of the verdict, I started pregaming that afternoon even before RTJ's bus broke down. I drank a sixer at home, listening to the amazing Run the Jewels 2 and following the unfolding developments via Twitter, and then I hit a bar not far from where RTJ's in-store appearance would have been. I drank several more beers and maybe a shot or two, but I was entirely too wrapped up in all that was going on to get very drunk. It's difficult for a brother of a certain size to get drunk on mostly beer anyway.

As I was sitting there attempting to get wasted and watching cable news on a muted television, with Makonnen's "Tuesday" blaring in the background, I looked out the window and saw several cop cars whizzing by, headed towards Clayton, where the courthouse is. I saw on the news where they had the perimeter to Clayton blocked off, not unlike when President Bush used to visit. I lived not far from there during the Bush years, and the Secret Service used to put roadblocks up right out in front of my house. Supposedly, it was based on some purely arbitrary radius they were required to secure. The announcement was made at UMSL, my mom's alma mater, which is closer to Ferguson.

There was a lengthy-ass preamble before the guy making the announcement said that Darren Wilson wouldn't be indicted, but CNN's chyron gave it way. It said that Wilson had been told earlier in the day that he didn't need to be there that evening to turn himself it. It's almost as if they knew before the grand jury had arrived at a verdict what the verdict would be, like they could have just as easily told Darren Wilson that a few weeks prior.

The verdict, as I recall, had been reached towards the end of the week before, but they didn't announce it until way late in the evening that Monday.

The idea behind this may have been to give Darren Wilson plenty of time to skip town, lest someone on Black People Twitter found out where he was, and to make it so there weren't as many people out in the street, in Ferguson. It was warmer that Friday, but it had been cold before then. It got cold again Monday and it was even colder at night.

What little I could gather from the pre-verdict spiel, on a muted television, seemed to have to do with discrediting the witnesses, which was the stated justification for not indicting Darren Wilson. Many of the witnesses, it was reported, gave conflicting accounts. Some people who told media they'd seen Mike Brown raise both his hands changed their story or admitted they hadn't actually witnessed the shooting.

Aspects of Wilson's story, like the idea that Mike Brown and Dorian Johnson fit the description of robbery suspects that went out over the dispatch, were obviously BS, but he at least had the sense to pick one story and stick to it the entire time. And this wasn't the actual trial anyway. All that was necessary here was to discredit the witnesses. If they succeeded, there'd be no trial.

There was maybe an hour between the announcement and when RTJ hit the stage. We took off for the venue, a new place in a (very) gradually gentrifying area with a lot of gay bars, much larger than anywhere I'd seen Killer Mike or RTJ before, but not huge by any means, this being St. Louis and all. Later on the same tour, they'd open for Jack White and bring out Zach de la Rocha at Madison Square Garden.

We got there in time to catch both of the headliners. Despot and Ratking. Despot came out complaining about not having time to fix his combover. Like El-P, you can't tell when he's being sincere. All the while, I was checking my phone for reports that Ferguson had been burned to the ground.

Later I read that there weren't as many livestreams, streamers having been told to stay away because 5-0 might be out there shooting people for filming. It's likely that many of the rioters were protest tourists and anarchists, like the ones who caused so much damage in Occupy Oakland

I saw more pictures of things burning than clashes with police. Later at home, I saw the video of people attempting to flip a car and then burning it and pictures of buildings on fire. It seemed as if 5-0 was purposely taking a hands off approach, as long as rioting was confined to the strip of businesses, some of which were black-owned, a block or two from the police station. The cops, I'm assuming, posted up between that strip and the station and intimated that they'd shoot anyone who even tried to approach. There's no way they wouldn't have gotten away with it.

RTJ took the stage to complete silence. They'd been coming out to "We Are the Champions," but as Killer Mike explained in his speech, he didn't feel that would be appropriate; they didn't feel like champions. They felt like they'd just taken an L. Though I don't think any of us were surprised at the result of the grand jury trial. I could sense from the moment they took the stage that I was witnessing a historic moment, like Jimi Hendrix playing "The Star Spangled Banner" at Woodstock, and I hoped someone was recording. I looked around and didn't see anyone recording. How odd would it have been if something like that happened and no one thought to record it, at a time when so many of these police killings of mostly unarmed black men are being caught on video? As it turns out, someone was recording. By the time I got home, I saw where the video was circulating on Twitter. I posted a link to it myself. By the time I rolled off the couch the next morning, it was quite literally all over the Internets.

Killer Mike says he considered taking the stage to "Burn This MF Down," from Pl3dge, inspired in part by the police killing of Oscar Grant, as depicted in the brilliant Fruitvale Station. I visited Killer Mike in the studio during the recording of Pl3dge and suggested he work with El-P, though he has no recollection of this, possibly due both to weed and aging. At the time, I suspected the weed—which he forced me to smoke—was laced with PCP, like in Training Day, but I was later assured that it was just weed, albeit especially good weed, and I'm just a lightweight because I don't fuxwit weed, because I'm all about making good decisions. Obviously.

Both Killer Mike and El-P attempted to play their pre-RTJ stuff on the first RTJ tour, on which I was allowed to go on stage and promote my second book, Infinite Crab Meats, which had a chapter on RTJ before RTJ was even a group, and none of the kids there, who were probably like eight when that shit came out, knew what that shit was. And their audience has only gotten worse since then. They're now featured on Jezebel. They were doing RTJ stuff only on this tour.

Killer Mike says rather than play "Burn" he decided to consult the Google for a quote by MLK, which is what everyone's dumb aunt on Facebook does every time something bad and/or important happens. Famously, a quote falsely attributed to MLK circulated Facebook as if it was Farmville after bin Laden was assassinated. I'll spare you my thoughts on the bin Laden assassination other than to point out that I've been told that immediately dumping someone in the ocean isn't even a thing in Islam, I heard that something like 18 of the 20 guys involved in the raid died in a helicopter crash shortly thereafter, and the guys who survived have conflicting stories, both of which seem full of shit.

Looking for a quote by MLK, Killer Mike was struck by the fact that MLK was 39 years old when he died, the same age Killer Mike was that night. If he'd clicked through to the wiki he would have found that not only was MLK born in Atlanta, just like Killer Mike, but his Christian name at birth was Michael. The similarities are uncanny! MLK was the greatest black leader of his time. Arguably, Killer Mike is the greatest black leader of our time, in an admittedly less talented field. Who had a more astute take on Ferguson that night? I rest my case.

Maybe Killer Mike is less concerned with asinine coincidences than I am. Rather than turning up the quote about how it's inappropriate to rejoice in the death of your enemy, which wouldn't be in the wiki because it's fake and Wikipedia is the world's most accurate encyclopedia, Killer Mike seized on the fact that MLK was assassinated—probably by the FBI—because he came out in favor of ending the war and eradicating poverty, and if there's two things the government can't have, it's the end of war and poverty... not necessarily because they're in favor of starving children and dead Asians, but because that's how they make their money.

In that sense, what happened to Mike Brown wasn't altogether different from what happened to MLK. Yeah, he stole those cigarillos, and he wasn't necessarily someone you'd select to represent the black community, though he'd pass for Killer Mike in a pinch. Darren Wilson wouldn't have bothered with him in the first place if cops didn't troll the hood looking for black kids to harass, and the reason they do that, as one of the faux intellectuals from Gawker's weekend essay series might put it, is because they need black bodies to fuel the prison-industrial complex, one of the few growth industries left in this country, especially if you don't count the Silicon Valley startup scene, which is all fake. As Diddy warned in the movie Made, the bubble is about to burst.

As Killer Mike points out on "Reagan" from R.A.P. Music, the 13th amendment prohibits slavery unless you're in prison, in which case fuck it. Go hog wild! And so they've got guys in prison taking hotel reservations, manufacturing office furniture and what have you for like a dollar an hour. And it's likely they wouldn't give them that dollar if they didn't need it to buy soap. Otherwise they'd be walking around smelling like shit. Legally, they don't have to give you that dollar. And as Michelle Alexander points out every third page or so of The New Jim Crow, there's more black men in prison now than there were slaves during slavery, so slavery didn't go away so much as it got bigger than it ever was, albeit not relative to the size of the overall population, and granted it took a hundred years or so to get this point.

Interestingly, if you look at a graph of the explosive growth in the prison population since Richard Nixon declared war on drugs in the early '70s, it actually plateaued in the past couple of years. This is not because the police realized the error of their ways but rather because they've run out of room in the prisons they have and they can't afford to build new ones just yet. Tax revenue has been for shit since the economy fell apart in '08. In places like California and Arkansas, and probably many other states as well (those are just the ones I read articles about), they're constantly having to let people out before their sentence is up to make room for newer and/or more violent criminals.

This might be a good thing if all you did is smoke a little weed, which is legal now in some places. There's people in prison here in Missouri doing 30-year bids for marijuana possession, but how many more people can we afford to lock up for just weed? It costs more money to lock someone up for a year than it does to send him to Harvard, but good luck trying to argue that in court.

But it's definitely a bad thing for the privatized prisons and companies that use prison slave labor to manufacture their products or answer the phone. In the past, they've had problems making sure their beds were full, which is a problem for them since they get paid on the number of guys they've got spending the night, if you will. This led to the passing of laws which guaranteed the police would arrest enough people to keep private prisons at least 90% full, and if they don't taxpayers have to kick in the difference. Ridiculous as those laws are, that's no longer an issue anyway. The problem now is that if they can only hold but so many prisoners and they can't build any more facilities, growth will remain stagnant and the price of the stock might go down. It could ruin the whole economy!

I wouldn't be surprised if the next growth opportunity in the incarceration sector won't be more private prisons but rather concentration camps. There's bound to be more unrest in our cities, as cops kill more and more oftentimes unarmed black men for no apparent reason. In the month of March 2K15 alone, a good six months after the Mike Brown shooting and before it got warm out, US cops killed more people than UK cops killed in the entire 20th century.

More and more cop killings lead to more and more anti-cop sentiment, plus rioting when the cops get away with it. The National Guard will need places to put people if rioting is any more widespread than it was in Ferguson, where it was pretty much confined to one city block, or if militant factions of the Black Lives Matter movement declare war on the police and it's necessarily to lock people up preemptively, at least until they can figure out who poses a threat and who doesn't. The ongoing saga of Gitmo, which Obama promised to close when he took office, should give you an idea of how long that will take.

Hillary Clinton, who could be the next president (god forbid), was advocating "fun camps for adults" on the campaign trail before she even officially announced that she was running. Could it be that she knows something that we don't?

ACKNOWLEDGMENTS

The author wishes to acknowledge the makers of Pabst Blue Ribbon, the source of his creativity; the lovely ladies of RackRadar, for keeping him in Pabst Blue Ribbon and also for giving him a reason to get out of bed in the morning; El-P, who let him into that Run the Jewels show for free and only tried to hold it over his head when the author said something truly indefensible (if you can imagine); Combat Jack, for the title; Theotis Jones, who did the (brilliant) cover and illustrations; the people who copped Beatings by Dr. Dre and his five other books, for being part of The Resistance; and the people who signed up for his free, weekly email newsletter Life in a Shanty Town, at tinyletter.com/byroncrawford.

ABOUT THE AUTHOR

Byron Crawford is the founder and editor of the legendary hip-hop blog ByronCrawford.com: The Mindset of a Champion and a former columnist for XXL magazine. He lives in a shanty town.

Made in the USA
San Bernardino, CA
26 August 2015